Lady Ana

A memoir of an inner demon

By

Rhonda Straw

I wasn't loud so no one could even guess.

© 2022 By Rhonda Straw

ISBN: 979-8-218-06543-0

"Your eating disorder is not named Ana or Mia or Ed.

Your eating disorder is not your friend or your buddy

or a dietician helping you get skinny.

The only thing that you're eating disorder *is* is a mental disorder.

Pro-ana is not even a thing.

Saying you're pro-ana is like

saying you're pro-depression, pro-anxiety, pro-bipolar.

You don't want to be anorexic.

Want to lose weight? Go on a fucking diet. Exercise.

But don't *ever* say you *want* an eating disorder

like anorexia. It will ruin your life in the blink of an eye."

--Anonymous. (pro-ana boards)

Disclaimer

I support the recovery of the individual when they are ready to be treated and will never support those who seek to start an eating disorder. I use the term "Ed," not as a male name. ED is a medical abbreviation for *Eating Disorder*. I use the term "Ana" as a female name but not a radiant being. She's more of an angel of darkness. *Ana* is internet slang for anorexia. During my career in the '90's as a hospital floor nurse, it was somewhat common to see the term "*ana*" documented in a medical chart when a patient was anorexic. "*She's ana*," written in scrawled letters in the patient's progress notes.

This book is my own experience. It is for support of those who have anorexia and or bulimia and for those who are interested in the subject of eating disorders. My course is my course. I would never suggest anyone use the actions I write about in these pages. This is not a medical book to diagnose an eating disorder.

This is based on personal fact and actual experiences. I meant to include graphic, descriptive details. I wanted this to be in your face and concrete. It has fictional and character composites and names. Names of locations were changed to protect the innocent.

Preface

This is an account of my own personal experience. I am not excluding any repulsive details. My eating disorder ran in phases between 18 and 27, with several crushing relapses. There's one notable fact about the path I followed to anorexia and bulimia. My eating disorder fought against me. My eating disorder failed. If "failed" sounds pessimistic, I never reached success. I wanted my weight to be 95 pounds. A failed eating disorder to some is death. I wasn't looking for death. I was looking for the emaciated image of 95 pounds.

During adolescence, "Ana" groomed me into her realm of a mental disorder. Ana taught me to believe 95 pounds was a magic number. "Ana" and her partner "Mia" accompanied me at the age of 18, after I graduated high school. The goal of 95 pounds flowed throughout my thoughts and visions. The word *ninety-five* affected a cheerleader in high school. She "got down to 95 pounds" (according to high school gossip, and probably down to 85 pounds). She was admitted to the hospital. 95 pounds was the ultimate challenge and the number of **success**, but the cost, was failure.

While I displayed picky eating issues and later, eating disorder symptoms, I didn't have sufficient recovery therapy. I wasn't labeled "sick enough" to be hospitalized. I didn't collapse, as in the many sugar-coated Hollywood movies, television shows or sometimes in real life. My BMI didn't get low enough to qualify for recovery therapy.

In my situation the magic number of 95 never materialized. The lowest BMI of 18 was far out of reach.

In Internet forums, you'll find "passing out and collapsing" is a reality and also scale numbers lower than the magical 95 pounds. At least that's what girls post in forums. Yes, they are *usually* girls, but guys aren't eliminated. They maintain the low weight. Yet 95 pounds and lower is challenging to maintain without a crisis. While some runners and sports figures are low weight, maintaining a low weight with an eating disorder is destructive.

There are horrific side effects of anorexia and bulimia. I've not ruptured my esophagus or had a prolapse of any type from either end of my digestive system. An esophageal prolapse is a rare possibility with bulimia. Rectal prolapse, though not as common, has been reported while overdosing on laxatives (NCBI, 1997). Gastroesophageal reflux disease or GERD, irritable bowel syndrome and electrolyte imbalance can result from both types of eating disorders. These three conditions are more common, as are abdominal distension, altered esophageal motility, and laxative addiction. Not to mention the embarrassment of passing out in public from electrolyte depletion. Teeth problems are a real danger with bulimia. Stomach acid and the presence of hydrochloric acid in the mouth cause tooth enamel erosion, hoarseness, dental caries, soft palate damage, cracked or missing teeth and salivary gland enlargement (Ekron, 2018) .

One of the signs of anorexia is a lowered serotonin level. Serotonin is metabolized from food. With bulimia present, there is a significant drop in serotonin levels. The disorders also affect dopamine. In anorexic patients, the serotonin is lower in the cerebrospinal fluid. It is thought that starvation causes a person with anorexia to feel better. But as they continue to starve, the supply of serotonin is drained. Once treatment is started, serotonin builds up and is replaced. At this point, the levels increase and cause anxiety and emotional discord. (nationaleatingdisorders.com, 2016)

Eating disorders should not be taken lightly. I wrote this book to warn anyone who not only decides to experiment into the route of bulimia, but also anorexia, to get inside the world of eating disorders and know how disgusting the path feels, smells, looks, appears and other associated adjectives. To even play around with each disorder can result in something worse.

My BMI briefly, meaning maybe a week or more, tilted quite low. Looking back, I can't say I'm pleased. I STILL feel like my eating disorder failed.

How would I have looked? What size clothes would I buy? Would my ribs be more protruded? I still regret that I was never thin *enough* and why, you ask? Anorexia causes these thoughts: "Smaller sized clothes are cuter and more feminine. Thinner looks better and is certainly healthier."

That's the danger of a life with eating disorders, the thought process that rolls around in the brain, gnawing and creating these concepts.

My ambition was to get a thigh gap; like many photoshopped pictures that are viewed in Google images today under the search word *anorexia*. I wanted thin legs, almost like twigs or bones. Thigh gaps are often a result of a good Photoshop editor unless a woman is in excellent shape and has an extremely low BMI as are "*thinspiration*" photos. One of my friends. Ambre has a thigh gap. My envy is sickening.

Let me explain that term. "*Thinspiration*" became popular on the internet before *online* became a household compound word.

During the late '80s, primitive websites began to emerge just as the internet began to flourish. Bulletin boards were dial-up and ran by people in their home. Scant number of websites from the late '80s posted pictures of thin women. Though there were plenty of pornography websites, *thinspiration* sites also began to increase. These women did not have a pornography stance. *Thinspiratio*n photographs represented women overly thin, what some would describe as having "Perfectly thin bodies." The online pictures were usually in .jpg format (JPEG stands for Joint Photographic

Experts Group and are the standard image file for computers). In the '80's you had to copy the photographs to a floppy drive. The hard disk didn't have sufficient memory for .jpg files. There was a payment for some of the pictures to be downloaded and saved.

In the late '80s, online *thinspiration* photos weren't as plentiful as in the coming years but were available if one knew where to look. To find *thinspiration*, a home computer owner needed some technical knowledge, a dial-up modem, and a phone line for online services such as AOL or CompuServe. Technical expertise was a requirement, and like today, not just a phrase. As computers and internet evolved to the present, it became easier to find *thinspiration* photos.

Thinspiration photos displayed pictures of women's skinny ribs, spines, abdomen, butts, arms, legs, depression poses, full length clothed, full-length bikini, body facing toilets, etc. The pictures were and are meant to *trigger* anorexia or bulimia. But they can also trigger false anorexia. False anorexia can lead to problems for those attempting to mimic the condition. The street term for false anorexia is loosely called *Wannaerxia*. It's not a term I've used. Anyone wishing to have anorexia and follows the path *is* already disordered.

EDNOS is "eating disorder not otherwise specified" and is as severe as anorexia and bulimia. In 2017, the new DSM V (*Diagnosis and Statistical Manual of Mental Disorders*) has a few new diagnoses for other conditions not specified. *Thinspiration* efficiently targets girls who's eating disorder might be classified as EDNOS but can evolve to clinical anorexia nervosa.

In the '90s with better computers, Yahoo Groups started popping up online that discussed anorexia, low BMI, meal plans, purging, recovery, relapse, tricks, and tips. They often contained pro-ana *triggers* called *Thinspo*. *Thinspo* is, in essence, a term for *thinspiration*. The groups were called "Pro-Ana groups," and Yahoo liked to delete them. But soon these groups found their way to websites, Pinterest, internet forums and Tumblr. There's even *thinspiration* on Reddit. Google search "*Thinspiration*" and you'll see hundreds of websites. Change the search to images, and there are thousands of pictures. Tumblr is a significant culprit.

Yahoo made searching for diets easy. Pro-ana eating lists exist today and can easily be found on Google.

"Triggers" are very dangerous for people with anorexia. *"Triggers are a word, phrase, picture, movie, anything that sets an eating disorder in place."* (Eating-disorders glossary)

Some thinspiration photos are so disgusting they do nothing towards the trigger mechanism. But most do the trick especially if there's a mental problem. I discuss at length my triggers in the following chapters. The internet, with the good it provides, can be a huge trigger even for relapsing. If someone with an eating disorder wants to search, there's always a way to find a trigger, and she or he knows where to look.

"Ed" is the slang for eating disorder. The abbreviation isn't street jargon, but it has taken an appearance of a catchy "secret term" in the pro-ana sect.

"Ana" is short for anorexia and began to take off as a term as the internet began hosting pro-ana sites. It was created by its victims. "Ana" makes the condition sound attractive and feminizing. It's *not* attractive. Anorexia is not *wanting* just to be thin. And it's not *just* a medical abbreviation. There is a line between a diet and an eating disorder. Ana isn't a diet. ED isn't a male's name.

A *diet* is not disordered eating though some diets disguise themselves, especially diets that restrict calories to the amount of 500 a day. I can name several I've tried. You might as well look up "pro-ana" on the internet, because that's where you'll find all of the 500 calorie diets. 500 calories a day sucks. 500 calories make your body feel like shit. Yet, it's maintained.

There is always an *underlining cause* in an eating disorder. Eating disorders are a *mental condition*. Ana and Mia disguise as thin and pretty, or not good enough. It is a scale or measurement someone can reach. Reading this sounds nice, something reachable, a size 5, thin waist, delicate, waiflike; eating disorders aren't elegant or filled with glamor. A woman can be a size 5 and be fine. It's a paradox.

I am writing to remove the glamorization. If eating disorders aren't diagnosed in time, they can become fatal or wreck your life. I'm lucky to be typing this book. Often eating disorder stories don't have a happy ending. If they do have a happy ending, it's overplayed. Most eating disorder stories, books or movies, or all I've read, entail expensive therapy and ends with the woman cured and happy, or dead. They are solely written to trigger. This book can trigger as well.

I'm mad at Ana and Mia. It is still tempting, when I get depressed, to go right back into the bathroom and shove my finger down my throat after I eat. If I'm triggered, I do it, especially if I eat what I consider to be "too much food."

Now it's fucking Slim Tea or cleanses because those are accepted, and in fact, those are encouraged. "Try Slim Tea if you're constipated from the diet. It always works. You'll lose a few pounds, too." I'm mad at Slim Tea. And I'm *pissed* at my eating disorder. Even major diet services make their own brand of Slim Tea. I was offered it recently. I glared at the girl. The look in my eyes could shoot out nails from my pupils. Slim Tea contains senna, it's a fucking laxative. Don't offer that shit to me.

My story isn't one of those where the girl turns up dead or cured, and I decided to write this because there are people who can't afford treatment, others don't want treatment and hide anorexia. This is how they live their lives. This is anorexia and bulimia without treatment.

Notes

I am a nurse, and I know better than to take this route. This book can trigger but does not make the condition charming. It's not my fault if this triggers someone as they chose to read the contents. Add to this condition, bulimia, which is a hidden, repulsive *monster*. It is a *sickness*. It is *disgusting* when written from the truth. I have never read anything that places bulimia where it belongs. Anorexia, as a disease model, is a bearcat to control, and very difficult to treat from a medical standpoint. It's also easily hidden from medical professionals. I managed, from 18 to27 to hide the condition.

The word "*anorexia*" means "Loss of appetite." The word "*nervosa*" adds the pathological fear of weight gain, indicating a lower-than-normal BMI. When adding "nervosa" to "anorexia," the term becomes a clinical travesty. Anorexia nervosa is not a condition someone *wants*. What an average person *wants* is a diet that will make them thin, without struggle. This is the difference in an anorexic and normal diet mindset.

Anorexia can cause hair loss and hormone depletion. It causes amenorrhea which is a loss of menstrual period. (I was never that lucky. In anorexia, amenorrhea is due to low body weight. It can lead to cardiac arrest or osteoporosis. When a girl visits her physician with issues of being underweight, doctors try everything, including thyroid tests, when in truth; the problem is an eating disorder, and it's not *just* "eating disorder."

Some doctors still don't recognize these disorders unless the BMI is below average. The healthy levels of a normal BMI range from 19-22. Physicians and insurance companies frown on a BMI above 22. Insurance companies don't recognize these as disorders if the BMI isn't low enough and deny reimbursement claims. The treatment costs thousands and is often ineffective, as the condition relapses. The definition of *low enough* on the BMI scale is below 18. For a woman 5 foot 1, BMI of 18 is below 98 pounds. On a woman 5 foot 4, BMI of 18 is 100 pounds. (Watson, 256stuff.com) It's easy to get caught up in a fight with the BMI scale and stay low enough to maintain the number of 19. BMI is not indicative of an eating disorder, that's a misconception.

Bulimia ("Mia") is the horrific side of anorexia. Both are life-threatening. Bulimia is the act of purging after eating. Often bulimics binge on food then "*get rid of it*." Some doctors think, "If you don't binge, and you eat normally, then you don't have bulimia." That phrase is misguided. I would correct the statement and say, "If you are purging after you eat, and do this regularly for two to three months, you are developing bulimia."

Bulimic girls are often at BMI, or slightly above due to calories from food being consumed and absorbed. Their BMI might be classified as obese. They may be 160 pounds and 5 foot 4. People can't judge from appearance if a person is bulimic. It's the act of purging that diagnoses the disorder. Age is no indication, either, as they might be 40-year-old women, not young girls.

Only 60% of patients are successful in treating eating disorders with a full recovery. (mirror-mirror.org) 20% of people with severe eating disorders succumb to the disorder itself. Anorexia becomes deadly when clinicians add the word *nervosa* to the diagnosis. Anorexia by itself is loss of appetite, but when discussing the disorder, it's known as "*Anorexia*".

When accepting a patient into treatment, BMIs need to be lower than 18 to be classified as a clinical mental illness requiring therapy. A BMI of 17 grants you better treatment if you have the cash. Also, eating disorders don't discriminate age or weight. A woman can be in her 40's, 50's, 60's and have anorexia or bulimia. It also effects men but is more common in women. The clinical classification needs to be changed so that all of those affected can seek proper treatment.

One month of performing the act of anorexia, which is eating at a very low caloric deficit, the person might start at 170 pounds and end up around 150 pounds being praised by society. It's a problem that needs to be rethought in medical teaching.

Once I heard a well-known doctor on TV tell a woman her disordered eating was not disordered at all. When this problem occurs, yes, it is disordered eating, and most likely is EDNOS. (Eating Disorder Not Otherwise Specified.) If someone thinks they have an eating disorder, doctors shouldn't deny the problem. EDNOS is not a joke. As I mentioned earlier, it is just as dangerous as the other major disorders. EDNOS is what they diagnose if there are no defining traits of other diseases.

There are no numbers of how many people *don't* seek help or report eating issues to their practitioner. This could be due to embarrassment, or in my case, wanting to keep the connection to the disorder itself. Then there is a matter of money. Not to mention insurance not covering the issue due to a higher BMI.

Admitting to others is scary because the person doesn't want to stop the disordered eating. The eating disorder controls the victim, and then they want to own it as theirs. Some that seek help obtain an incompetent therapist, and both time and money are wasted. The disorder becomes a dangerous defense mechanism. To me, I think anorexia/bulimia reminds me of an alcohol as addiction. Lack of food is the quotient. Too much food is a disaster.

People with past eating disorders always have the disorder, but it can be controlled. Control is learned in therapy, but I've read of too many relapses, and personally, I don't trust a therapeutic program if only a few therapy sessions are required.

Anorexia and or bulimia is occasionlly linked to a genetic imbalance of chromosomes 1 and 10 (eatingdisorderhope.com). Whatever the cause, if treatment is sought then there is a possibility for success.

The current BMI standards:

Below 18.5-Underweight

18.5-24.9-Normal

25-29.9-Overweight

30-39.9-Obese

Over 40-Morbidly Obese

Basic Glossary:

Anorexia: A lack of appetite

Anorexia nervosa: A serious brain disorder that has the potential of becoming deadly. Anorexia Nervosa is characterized by self-starvation or excessive exercise. One of the signs of anorexia nervosa is restricting calories. It includes distorted body image thinking. It can cause cardiac arrest, osteoporosis, depression, death. It is medically referred to as "AN." Its sufferers refer to it as "Ana".

Binge Eating Disorder: Excessive binge eating without purging.

Bulimia: a serious eating disorder that usually occurs in females. Bulimia is characterized by eating with self-induced vomiting or laxative abuse.

Bulimia Nervosa: This kind of disorder occurs with binge eating and compulsory behavior. Non-purging is binging and compulsatory exercising. There can be compulsive starvation following a binge. Of course, the purging type is included in this category.

Disordered Eating: describes irregularities in eating patterns.

DSM: Diagnostic and Statistical Manual of Mental Disorders. In 2017, DSM V was published.

ED-NOS: Eating Disorder Not Otherwise Specified. DSM IV describes this as individuals who don't meet the qualifications of other eating disorder diagnosis.

Orthorexia: Preoccupied with eating healthy food as a disorder. This term is not included in the DSM IV. I include this term cause of the existence and popularity of organic or raw food diets.

Purging: The use of self-induced vomiting, diuretics, laxatives after eating to prevent weight gain.

(NEDA, 2017)

(2017, March 22). Retrieved from

https://www.nationaleatingdisorders.org/learn/glossary

Chapter 1

EARLY CHILDHOOD

I am an only child, and close to my family. I was adopted at birth and consider my adoptive parents, my parents. My mom, May is, 5 foot 1, with a beautiful heart. She is very loving, giving and concerning. She is a kind person with a gracious spirit. My dad, Hal, was tall, 6 foot 2, robust, with tan skin and tattoos from the military. Dad died in 2009 of kidney failure. Serving in the Korean War, he was proud of America. A remarkable person, loving and kind, he was the most magnificent dad any adopted child or any child would want. I love him dearly.

We were a dog family. Throughout life, I always had a dog. When I was younger, I had Pete, a Jack Russel terrier. He was such a loveable dog. He slept either at the foot of my bed on the floor or cuddled up in a blanket in my bed at night. He played fetch and was very well trained. He was a show dog and walked with a strut. He liked to run and was great on a leash.

We lived in Savannah, MO where I grew up. Savannah had a lot of open spaces, trees that were beautiful during the change of seasons, and quaint little shops in the town square. Savannah is known for the Stoney Brook Farm, a three-million-dollar property that looked like a billion-dollar estate from the air. Savannah had rolling green hills and beautiful parks with jungle gyms, swings, and softball fields.

Trees outlined hills that looked like multiple color of green mountains in the summer. In the fall, the shadow of orange, brown and gold peered from the hills of trees onto the streets. The Hundred and Two River flowed into the Platte River and ran parallel to the Missouri River. Our family used to go fishing on the Platte River. In the summer, dad packed a fishing boat, and the four of us, dad, mom, me and Pete with his harness and leash, and rode the boat on the river. It was a quiet river, hardly any current. I used a life preserver and Pete usually laid on the floor of the boat. Sometimes a fish would jump out of the water, or a goose would dive down and grab a meal. Trees and trails lined the Platte River. We fed fish slices of bread from the boat. Dad parked the fishing boat and found trails among the trees, with wildflowers peeking out of blossoms. Once, Pete chased a brown fox. I'd see the occasional crane or hawk flying above.

Savannah was about 45 minutes from the Loess Bluff Wildlife Refuge. 300,000 geese flew and migrated all at once in a symphony of squawks and feathers. The geese flew in large numbers, with a whish in the air that could be felt while observing them migrate. I always looked for bald eagles and saw a few, plus a nest. In a child's eyes, it seemed magical.

Savannah was a peaceful town, mostly farmland. It contained a town square, a few churches, and graveyard and a Chevrolet dealership.

Chapter 2

BEGINNINGS

On a map, Savannah was a tiny dot often overlooked without a magnifying glass. It was approximately 20 minutes northeast of St. Joseph. It was half an hour south of Maryville.

    The sound of wind sweeping through oak, maple and elm trees and dogs barking in quiet neighborhoods gave Savannah a peaceful feeling. Smells of fresh bouquets of roses, tulips and jonquils highlighted the senses. In the center of town were historic buildings made of red bricks.

    Savannah's town square thrived in the early years. Towards the eighties, the square declined. Stores closed, which sometimes happens in smaller towns. A few businesses continued to operate. Antique stores lined the main street of town housed in old red brick buildings. Many of the roads through Savannah were one way and a few made of cobblestone. Many pleasant memories from early years in Savannah are fresh in my mind.

I have no knowledge of my birth. Due to my adoption, there is no medical history. I had zero hereditary descriptions until getting a DNA test in 2016. I carry gene #rs17496827 for eating disorders, foretelling a 30% chance. Another gene that's in my tracking system is one that gives me 42% chance of having anorexia, gene # rs2383378..

Children who are adopted sometimes suffer from undiagnosed mental issues, unknown to anyone, even themselves. Closed adoptions open up an entirely new gene tracking system that wouldn't be needed if adoption laws changed the regulations. They are improving but the laws aren't updated yet. The only hereditary affliction I currently display and have had all my life is a terrible case of allergies. My allergies consist of feathers, chocolate, eggs, some nuts, non-processed dairy including milk, seasonal allergies, and dust and mold. As an adult, I can't get a flu shot due to a couple of scares of anaphylaxis in 1998 and in 2002.

My birthday is March 7, 1962. My parents led full, social lives. My mom bowled with a few women of the neighborhood. My dad liked to play cards with the men while the women bowled. My mom was active in the church. We attended every week unless I was sick, which occurred several times a year. We belonged to the Savannah Christian Church. I went to the children's room in church while mom attended service in the sanctuary. I always thought the sanctuary seemed eerie, almost funeral-like in red and white tones. I was probably right in my feelings of the sanctuary, with all the funerals that took place inside. Dad often worked Sundays or stayed home to watch the Kansas City Chiefs.

We were a democratic family. My dad belonged to the Teamsters Union. He worked for the City of Savannah. My parents were vocally political, and I learned enough to never vote Republican and always exercise my right to vote, by 2nd grade.

I played with a tiny stove, refrigerator and sink with running water in a playroom in the house. I had a

Shrinking Violet and Betsy Wetsy doll. I still have a Chatty Cathy from my childhood. I saved her dress and kept her in good shape to display on my bookshelf. I also have a collectible doll; (mom called them "beautiful dolls") that sits on a pillow in a red velvet outfit with a red bonnet. I begged for a beautiful doll one Christmas. Though cost prohibitive, I received her as a Christmas gift. In the '70s. I also had a Chrissie doll whose hair grew.

    An early memory is going to a nearby 7-Eleven with my dad. I was four. That morning, he drove his City of Savannah truck, and I accompanied him. Accompanying my dad in the passenger seat of the city truck, he said, "Where do you want to go?"

    I said, "Let's go to 7-11."

Dad said, "Okay, I'll take you to 7-11."

I was wearing white flowered pajamas. Dad bought cigarettes and an Icee for me.

I remember critical events like Robert F. Kennedy's assassination and bits of news about Woodstock.

One early memory I have with my mom is going grocery shopping. It's odd that this memory is so clear. In 1967, six years old, the little Dell Purse books were prevalent at grocery counters. Titles like: "5 Day Diets," "Recipes for Weight Loss," "Exercise to a New Figure," "Lo-Gram Diets," "A New Figure in 30 Days," and the very popular "Count Your Calories." Each had a less attractive, often cheaply drawn or cheesy female model, in leotard and tights, presenting the title with her outstretched arms. *Count Your Calories* showed pictures of fruit in an abacus on the cover. Each book cost a quarter.

The book *"Count your Calories"* was a weak attempt at a calorie counter, with basic foods from the supermarket categorized in alphabetic order. I accompanied my mom to the grocery store, and these little books would find their way into the cart. That's exactly how I acquired *Count Your Calories*. I had read a lot of weight loss and calorie books by the time I was out of 6th grade, reading at an adult level.

I attended preschool at Busy Bee Preschool in Savannah. Every time my mom dropped me off, I cried for an hour in a corner. Busy Bee preschool was in a house where the teacher lived. It was a white painted house, with an area for kids built on the west side. Busy Bee had a large yard with a fence and a gate. It was full of medium-sized rooms. One room was large enough for fold out cots for napping. My mom brought a pillow with a pink pillowcase that matched a pink blanket for my naps. After naps, we were given cookies, and the teacher said, "these are freshly made cookies." I don't remember a fresh cookie smell.

Near Halloween in preschool, we got to decorate pumpkin shaped cookies. Mom was already teaching me to read, identify colors and numbers. In preschool, they taught us early reading, numbers, and colors as well.

My preschool teachers wore silver wire-framed glasses, hair pulled into a bun and loafers with house dresses and nylons. There were two preschool teachers and 15-20 students.

It was 1966, and Lyndon B. Johnson was president. Events began heating up in Viet Nam, and The

Beatles were more popular than Jesus. My mom stayed at home to take care of me, and my dad worked.

My mom bowled with my best childhood friend, Carla's, mother. We enjoyed sleepovers, with dolls. My Shrinking Violet said, "I have butterflies in my stomach." Carla's Thumbelina wound up and crawled across the floor. We pretended both dolls talked to each other. Shrinking Violet, though stuffed, had a moving mouth and eyebrows. We played with my play kitchen and made cakes in my Easy-Bake Oven.

Carla was little, almost frail. She had short brown hair, and we were friends for over three years. Carla and I climbed trees in the fall and made snow angels and snowmen in the winter. We became inseparable. This was when medical practitioners weren't highly technical. Carla complained to her mom of a sore throat and went to the hospital. The operation was a common tonsillectomy. She was gone for a week, then my mom received the worst news. Carla had to be placed in an iron lung due to respiratory failure, and that's where she died. Being that young, I felt the loss of a best friend but moved on.

I continued to be in and out of the doctor's office with staph infections, ear infections, and respiratory infections. I had eczema and constantly on avoidance diets to figure out what was wrong.

In 1967, my mom enrolled me in a dance class in Savannah during kindergarten. I loved dancing and had a natural rhythm to music. I attended dance class from kindergarten through 6th grade. There were ten to fifteen girls and two boys in my dance class. I wore a burgundy or teal leotard with white tights and pink or silver ballet shoes. I also took acrobatics. The older girls could do aerial cartwheels across the floor mat. Often, I thought, "How did they do that?"

Once I did cartwheels and backflips in the grocery store aisle, wearing a red and white dress and white patent leather shoes. The cartwheels I performed in the grocery store weren't as well received as the girls performing aerial cartwheels in dance class.

I learned ballet in dance class and practiced it at home with a 45 RPM record, *5 Positions All in a Row* by Kimbo. I loved everything about ballet. As a child, I enjoyed dance and movement. It defined part of me and made for physical activity since I abhorred competitive sports. I was afraid of competition, in fact, scared I might get hurt.

Chapter 3

KINDERGARTEN AND FIRST GRADE

My kindergarten class was in a church basement a mile from our house. I felt special in kindergarten because I got to leave once a week for allergy shots. Twice a year I had allergy tests, leaving twenty welts in my upper arm. I wore short sleeve t-shirts to cover the whelts. No one could figure out why I kept getting sick.

    I liked kindergarten. Morning and afternoon classes separated the time of kindergarten sessions. I was lucky to attend during morning hours. My kindergarten teacher would gather us around in a circle and read Little Golden Books. I developed an interest in reading, and almost every time my mom went to the grocery store, I slipped a Little Golden Book in the cart. My favorites were *Scuffy the Tugboat*, *Poky Little Puppy*, and *Little Black Sambo*. I thought Little Black Sambo was a farmer. He looked like a sweet little boy who lived in our neighborhood who's family-owned show horses.

Scuffy Tugboat looked like the boat on the Missouri river I saw when we rode over the bridge on the freeway. Poky Little Puppy was Pete. Each Little Golden Book had a character that seemed real.

I read a lot of Dr. Seuss. *One Fish, Two Fish, Red Fish, Blue Fish*; *Cat in the Hat,* and *Green Eggs and Ham* are classics still available today.

I attended state of the art, brand new elementary school. It opened in 1967. Inside were long modernized halls of hundreds of doors to classes. I'm not sure the count of the doors, but the building was long and narrow.

The library and offices separated the hallway of the school. Another hall of doors connected to the offices. In the middle of the school, the cafeteria doubled as a meeting room. The benches and tables folded down from the wall. PTA, school fairs, orchestra, and band concerts took place in the cafeteria. The gym was at the far end of the hall. The gym floor had a folding wall in the middle for separate classes or games.

In first grade, my doctor finally discovered what is still denied by a few medical professionals. I had a dairy allergy that wasn't lactose intolerance. My dairy allergy caused my throat to swell, along with coughing and gagging. It took many allergy tests, in and out of the clinic to discover the allergy. It was known in my medical record that I carried staph which caused inner ear infections. Doctors' visits were numerous. After a change of doctors and several visits, my newest doctor finally discovered that I had a lot of allergies, including milk and eggs.

The first time I was forced to drink milk at lunch was an awful experience! My mom sent me to school with green, lime Koolaide in my lunch box thermos. In the other side of my Barbie and Ken tin lunchbox with a matching thermos, she packed peanut butter and jelly sandwich and potato chips in Ziplock bags. I drank the green colored Koolaide, ate the packed lunch in the cafeteria.

My first-grade teacher, Mrs. Butler, insisted everyone drink milk at lunch. Mrs. Butler, an older woman, I presume in her '70's had gray hair pulled tightly in a bun. I think this hairstyle defined older women in Savannah clear through the '80s when hair coloring, style, clothing, and make-up became more prominent, especially if you had a job that required authority. My mother never wore her hair in that style. When I was seven, hair pulled back into a bun was "old lady hair" to me. The older women who were authoritative were probably twenty years behind my mother but looked fifteen years older.

Mrs. Butler gave everyone in the class a carton of milk. She showed a bewildered expression when my lunch didn't contain any of the magical protein. "You cannot be alive without drinking milk. Please, everyone, drink your milk, its good protein," she said to me and the class, peering over her silver wire-framed glasses. She sat at the end of the table in the cafeteria. She put a carton of milk in front of me, and I drank it. I remember wearing a lace lavender dress with white anklets and white Mary-Jane patent leather shoes.

    After lunch, we were rounded up in a single file line and walked back to the classroom. The bathroom was in the back of the room. Mrs. Butler was in the lead. Mrs. Butler instructed our class to use the bathroom and ordered us to get in line for recess. While standing in line to go to recess, I felt a pain in my stomach and dizziness. Suddenly I projectile vomited green Kool aid on the floor, other students, my lavender dress, white lace socks, and Mrs. Butler's black hose and black loafers. The school had to call my mom.

    Milk allergy brightly decorated my medical chart after this adventure, but some of the teachers didn't believe it existed. "Eat your ice cream honey," they would say. I could only tolerate so much ice cream before vomiting.

As an adult, milk, and sometimes ice cream, creates an asthmatic condition and a migraine. I carry an inhaler just in case. I have researched milk allergy and found a lot of dairy allergies are from the milk protein called casein. Being an allergy culprit, I try to avoid anything with casein as a stand-alone ingredient.

As an adult, I am reminded every year that I'm exempt from flu shots due to two scares of anaphylaxis. I was administered a flu shot in 1998 and started turning cyanotic within an hour. I spiked a temperature of 104. Flu shots contain eggs. The nurse forgot to ask if I had allergies. And this happened again in 2002. Even though they say the flu shot won't harm me, I'm afraid of it.

Two experiences with anaphylaxis leads to a lifetime of avoidance.

During the summer of first grade, my family went to Minnesota. They learned I wasn't such a great travel companion when I got car sick, repeatedly, in the family Cadillac. The second time they drove to Minnesota, I got to stay with my grandpa and grandma who owned a farm to the east of Savannah.

At the farm, we awakened early to the sound of the rooster. We got dressed and went outside to gather eggs. Grandpa taught me to milk cows. I stayed at the farm often. During hay baling season, usually in the fall, I worked hard and went to bed exhausted. Grandma cooked food for the guys who were bailing hay. I served the food to them, and also brought them water or coffee in thermoses. If they needed help with the hay, I wasn't useful but tried to help where I could. Grandpa had a barn he filled with hay and was able to feed the cows and pigs throughout the year.

Grandpa had two horses, cows, pigs, chickens, and a huge garden. I loved the piglets. I chased them, then cuddled and petted them. I picked them up and snuggled them. They loved to be petted just like Pete. Grandpa always had a dog and a couple of cats. His dog was a large farm dog, trained for herding. The cats, were, as Grandma explained, "Just some cats that wandered on the farm" We picked vegetables, and he loaded his truck to sell them at the Savannah Farmer's Market. Grandma made pies, fresh rolls and most important, her sweet corn and divinity candy. Grandma canned some of the vegetables Grandpa grew in the garden.

On the farm was a cellar made of cement where Grandma stored canned vegetables. Inside the cellar were cement shelves. The cellar was built into a grassy hill beside the house. They had 2 horses in a field beside the house and a large persimmon tree. Grandma canned persimmons as well.

Grandpa grew grapes and made his own wine. Grandma drew the wine labels. One time I was staying all night and Grandpa made wine and put it in jars in the refrigerator. Grandma had made a batch of root beer. The wine was the same color, at least in the dimly lit fridge. Grandma poured root beer for me, and wine for them. I was sitting in front of the wrong glass at the kitchen table and took a huge gulp of wine. It was *horrible*! I ran to the kitchen sink and spit it out. Grandpa and Grandma had a quite a laugh.

Chapter 4

BACH, MOZART AND DAYDREAMING

In second grade, I had to have weekly visits to a speech and reading therapist. I pronounced "sheep" like "thweep" and "writer" like "whitah." I pronounced my name, Rhonda like *Wanda*. My speech therapist, Mrs. Agnes Thwart, who tutored both speech and reading had grey hair pulled back into a tight bun. (Notice a pattern here?) She wore silver wire-framed glasses, and house dresses. Therapy was in her home. Her living room had a rust-colored couch, yellow chairs and a couple of lamps. Mrs. Agnes Thwart sat on the couch, and me on one of the yellow chairs.

During speech therapy sessions, Mrs. Agnes Thwart said, "Your name is pronounced RRRhonda. Purse your lips and say RRR," she said demonstrating how to pronounce R.

"WWWWanda," I repeated.

"No, RRRRRhonda."

After several visits, speech and reading therapy worked. I still have the book from speech and reading therapy. It's called *"More Times and Places."* I checked on Amazon, and it's $3.98.

In 2nd grade, I developed a habit of daydreaming and looking outside through the windows. I was shy. I couldn't approach anyone, therefore didn't make friends easily, nor use eye contact. In second grade I heard the teacher say too many times, "Rhonda look this way. Use eye contact. Over here," snapping her fingers for attention. Snap, snap. I heard this line from teachers throughout elementary school.

I read voraciously. Reading was quiet and effortless. Books took me places and allowed me to see the world through the eyes of the author. By fourth grade, I read at a seventh-grade level. In sixth grade, I read so fast, I managed to finish *"To Kill a Mockingbird"* in a week, leaving the class behind on chapter 3. I checked out a different book at the public library every two weeks.

I loved coming home from school, when Pete jumped as far as the doorknob to make sure it was me. He also sat in my room or didn't, while I learned to play the violin.

In 4th grade, I learned to play the violin. I played in the school's student orchestra. There were twelve students in the orchestra. The school band had over fifty students. I loved my music teacher, Mrs. Andor.

I excelled with the violin. By 6th grade, I played in the community orchestra. While I practiced violin, Pete would sleep by my foot, usually. If I hit a series of flat or sharp notes or screeched, he'd give me a dirty look, shake his head and leave the room. After practicing violin, I walked Pete every day.

Dad was given a piano from a City of Savannah customer he helped during a storm when I was in third grade. Playing the piano came naturally for me, except it was difficult to cross my right and left hands. I had coordination problems in grade school.

I loved playing Christmas carols on the piano even in June. If I were to repeat my music education, I'd learn to play the piccolo. I've always wanted to play the piccolo. For some reason, the piccolo reminds me of fairy tales, fairies, meadows, and magic, as in The Magic Flute by Mozart.

My first piano teacher taught classical music like Mozart and Beethoven. She taught by the book. Each book graduated to the next level. I ended with level five. I participated in piano recitals. One of the recitals I played Bach's "The Harpsichord Player," from John Schaum Book B. My piano teacher quit teaching when she had a stroke.

I was fortunate to find a second piano teacher who rearranged music on music ledger so I could play it. He played in a local rock band and taught piano and guitar in his shop. I learned to play Styx's *Come Sail Away* and the *Charlie Brown Theme Song* among others.

I participated in the high school choir, and the teacher (one of my favorite teachers) singled me out, "Rhonda, you have shifty eyes. Rhonda, look at me. Eye contact, everyone, please." Eye contact haunted me throughout elementary clear through high school. I felt inferior and it caused problems to arise.

I continued music through high school and into college. In high school, I participated in yearly music contests in Warrensburg, MO.

Chapter 5

BREASTS AND BULLIES

Fourth grade was my first encounter with bullies, including teachers to students. Nobody controlled the bullies; the teacher just shrugged her shoulders. I began to develop breasts and got teased and pushed in the chest. I hated confronting anyone and was very shy. My social disconnection and lack of eye contact worked to a disadvantage. I also had a butt that to me was the size of an elephant.

Every girl develops breasts. I wore a trainer bra. Too bad Victoria Secrets wasn't around; I could've displayed a fashion statement.

My trainer bra was fashion*less,* and I think the girls who pushed me in the chest were jealous. Honestly, my breasts weren't even A cups, nothing to be jealous about. I grew to hate my body the way it looked: breasts, thighs, and butt.

In dance and acrobats, *no* body shaming existed in my class. The teacher stopped anyone from criticizing other girls. "That's enough of that. You want to be in my class or not? If not, keep that up." (*That* being whispers of, "She looks fat in her leotard.") I enjoyed dance and came close to majoring in it in college. I quit in high school but found a private teacher in 1982 and stayed in dance till until 1990. I had different reasoning for signing up for dance class in 1982 than I did as a child.

My fourth-grade teacher was Mrs. Stinger. Mrs. Stinger had long blonde straight hair and wore conservative dresses. She wore Bandolino shoes with a slight heel. I believe her age was late '20's. My mom said, "She is young and new."

Three girls in my 4th-grade class who towered over me started ganging up and shoving me on the playground. Samantha, Jennifer, and Laurie were inseparable. They sat by each other in the cafeteria, their moms made sure they had class together. When Jennifer got a new blouse, Samantha got the same blouse in different colors. Laurie began to buddy with Mrs. Stinger early in the year.

"Mrs. Stinger, I like your shoes. Are they Bandolino's?"

"Thank you, Laurie. Why yes, they are. See class how Laurie noticed *my* Bandolino heels and complimented *me*? These shoes are very rare and are called *designer heels*." Mrs. Stinger said with a smile that we were supposed to react with admiration.

A few days later, Jennifer noticed Mrs. Stinger's dress. "What a pretty dress, Mrs. Stinger."

"Why thank you, Jennifer. What a kind compliment to *me*." Mrs. Stinger replied. It was sickening and enough sap to make a person's skin sticky.

"Class, notice how Samantha, Jennifer, and Laurie compliment *me*? If you want to join them, they are my top of the class." Inside the classroom, Samantha, Jennifer and Laurie were constantly paying attention to Mrs. Stinger. Everything she did they complimented her. Those girls were angels and could no nothing wrong. But outside on the playground, these three girls were terrorizing me.

They had long hair and were not particularly pretty or skinny, but they were tall. Their long hair had the same ponytail. The girls pushed me on the playground and teased me on the monkey bar. I wasn't very good at the jungle gym. At home I complained to my mom. "Mom, I'm not very good at the monkey bars at school."

She drove me to the playground on Saturdays, so I could practice. Practicing helped, took away the fear, and suddenly I was one of the best in the class, which infuriated Mrs. Stinger. When other kids got complimented for how good they were at the monkey bar, when she saw me improving, she frowned. She wanted me to fail, as long as Jennifer, Samantha and Laurie were in her class.

At home, I was busy practicing beginning violin. The shrill, out of tune notes made Pete leave the room, and most likely, my parents wanted to leave the house. I liked my violin but playing it every day, practicing one hour a day was arduous. I pushed through it. I went to a private teacher once a week. Then I went home and practiced. The songs weren't really composed music; they were practice bits that someone wrote. Scales, arpeggios, and melodies filled my room.

In fourth grade, I got blamed for things I didn't do in the classroom by other students. I believe the Jennifer, Samantha and Laurie started telling lies about me to Mrs. Stinger. The other kids heard and joined them. I learned to pretend to be invisible. I started biting my nails and developed an apprehensive personality. Being a quiet child, I didn't speak up to the girls. I did tell my mother, who told the teacher, who didn't believe me.

I also *tried* to tell the teacher. I still remember her shoulder shrug and blank stare from her desk when I tried tattling on the girls for pushing me. "So?" she said, cold and apathetic. "What am I supposed to do about it?" Then she pointed to the papers on her desk indicating she had better things to do. Being a new teacher, she couldn't handle the stress of the job.

Everything that happened in the class was apparently my fault. Usually, I got blamed for bizarre set-ups by other students. Someone wrote, even misspelled my name, *Ronda* without the H scribbled on the steel axel of the earth globe in pencil. It was a boy's writing, scribbly, but Mrs. Stinger wouldn't hear my argument. I never scribbled on, nor would I ever deface an earth globe. I loved the globe. The answer was simple, right in her face that I didn't write on the globe. Mrs. Stinger saw my name and moved me to a cubicle desk in the back of the room, separated from the students. I had to stay in the cubicle for the rest of the month. This caused the students to point and jeer when I walked by them in class.

A few weeks later, someone wrote my name in a dictionary, again without the H. I used the dictionary a lot. Mrs. Stinger saw my name and moved me to the cubicle desk again, only this time, I got sent to the principal's office. The principal yelled, "IF YOU DO IT AGAIN!" and slammed a ruler on the palm of his hand. I was afraid of being spanked. When I tried to tell him "I didn't do it," he slammed the ruler on the desk again.

I didn't write on the globe or in the dictionary in the first place, how could I do it again? Then why in the world would I get blamed all the time? Neither adult listened to me. I went home, told my mom. She talked to the principle and Mrs. Stinger, and I kept getting bullied. The more I told on the kids, the more I was pushed around. And Mrs. Stinger shrugged her shoulders and pointed to the stack of papers on her desk. Oh, she liked the girls who bullied me more than anyone in the class. She played favorites and tried to get people in the class to favor the three girls.

"Look at Samantha's new purse. Isn't it pretty? Samantha, is that real leather?" Instead of being angry, I hid my eyes.

To me, the concept is simple. If a student walks up to a teacher and says, "I'm being pushed around," it's probably not in a teacher's best interest to blow them off or fuck them over. Really act like you give a shit and do something about it. It took a lot of nerve for me to approach Mrs. Stinger, I was so quiet and shy I couldn't figure out how to speak up. When I did, she didn't care. I began to think, "Teachers must not care for their students." I started getting mad at Laurie, Samantha, and Jennifer, and thought of them as 'the three terrors'.

Mrs. Stinger was shocked when I smacked the hell out Laurie later in the year. I was getting stronger by practicing on the jungle gym every weekend. I got in trouble for it, sent to the principal and then targeted by the teacher for the rest of the semester. I received F's when I should've gotten B's. I gave up and stopped turning in papers even though they were finished. I'm glad I passed the fourth grade.

Mrs. Stinger quit teaching the next year. We received a letter in the mail reading:

"We regret that Mrs. Stinger quit teaching. She got a job closer to her home. We are honoring her at a reception. Please join us. And please RSVP." My mom explained what RSVP meant, and we didn't respond.

As an afterthought, in tenth grade, Samantha got pregnant and quit school. I laughed.

Chapter 6

I PRINT AND IT'S OKAY

Around 5th grade, my mom noticed I was uncoordinated. My parents took me to a rehabilitation center (RC) in Maryville every week to correct my incoordination. I went after school. I couldn't hold a pencil to learn cursive, which we were expected to be doing fluently back in 3rd grade. I couldn't jump rope, ride a bike or throw a ball. I couldn't bat a baseball or kick a kickball. I ran like a monkey flapping my hands. And I was gravely shy. I couldn't talk to anyone, just my friends. Approaching strangers was too demanding and talking to teachers, too difficult. I didn't like to be touched or have rough material against my skin. Coarse material included sweaters. They made my skin itch. My mom knew there was something wrong with me. I couldn't stand loud noises and complained.

"But mom, that hurts my ears," I said when she ran the vacuum cleaner. It sounded like a lawnmower.

"You have sensitive ears, honey. Cover them to block the noise, or leave the room," mom said.

While in school, I stared into space so much in class that my doctor gave me Ritalin. I was diagnosed with attention deficit disorder.

I also got out of class for allergy shots once a week, just like I did in kindergarten, all the way through sixth grade. I always asked the allergy doctor what shot I was getting "this time?". I had to read the vial, see the needle, and always watched him draw up allergy serum into the syringe. Some of the serums were yellow, some were clear. He showed me the vial and told what it contained. I read the words on the alcohol pad. I also watched while he gave me the shot in my upper arm. "Don't look, it won't hurt as much." I always looked. He was a pediatrician allergy specialist. A little sign hung on his office's wall:

"I love children

Yes I do

Boiled or broiled

Or in a stew."

At the RC, I got to play perception games, work with tools, play a primitive video game and climb bars. I enjoyed doing the activities and looked forward to the days I went to RC. I loved to read and write and demonstrated my aptitude to the therapists. I really just wanted to please an adult.

At RC the therapists were encouraging and kind. They called me smart and intelligent. They praised me for my efforts. I got to climb bars, and they laughed and named me Monkey, It a very kind compliment.

"Some of our kids are squirrels, and some are fish. We name each an animal, and you're our little monkey."

I liked being a little monkey. A large steel swimming tank took over an entire room at RC. They said, "it's for people whose muscles don't work like yours." Then they added, "You're a monkey. You climb the bars faster than we do. Don't worry, all of your muscles work."

I'm not sure it helped my inadequacies during gym class, still despising sports, especially competitive sports, but I did benefit from the activities and constant encouragement from the therapists.

RC was ten or twenty years above technology. One activity I did was to guide a dot into a hole on a computer screen using a video controller with a joystick. I quickly excelled in the dot activity.

"Hey monkey, you're doing great! Even I couldn't move the joystick that fast. I need your secret."

I remember answering, "You have to think where the dot is going to land before the dot gets away from your controller."

The therapist said, "Thanks for the tip. You're the most intelligent little monkey here."

"Maybe I really am," I thought and smiled on the inside. The therapists made me feel like a whole *celebrated* person.

They tried to teach me how to hold a pencil for cursive, and I said, "It hurts my hand, so I'm going to print."

And the therapist said, "Then don't worry about it. Cause I'm not. You're a printer and it's okay." She decided to work with me on printing, which worked out well. (I still print. I can't stand cursive writing.)

I was never forced to write in cursive again in elementary school. In junior high and high school, I took pride in my printing, circle dotting my I's and making swirls around my signature.

After each RC session, my mom and I ate all-you-can-eat pizza at a restaurant buffet. While attending

RC, I felt a lift in my self-esteem. I felt genuine and confident. I think that's the most critical aspect of the experience.

Chapter 7

PERIOD AT THE END OF THE SENTENCE

I enjoyed the next two years of school, fifth and sixth grade, except for one horrific aspect which I kept to myself. I continued playing violin in our small orchestra with Mrs. Andor as my teacher.

The first day of sixth grade, I started my period that morning. It was September 4th, 1973. I noticed a brown stain after dressing in my special first day of school outfit. I was wearing khaki-colored safari shorts and blouse with a matching belt. My mom washed out my shorts, and I changed and had to wear a thick, buldging Kotex with a Kotex belt under my outfit. The

Kotex stuck out of my clothes, and I couldn't wear fitted clothes anymore. The whole ordeal was crushing. Several years earlier, I learned about menstrual periods, so I wasn't shocked at my body, but the mess, the smell, the embarrassment was repulsive. Again, I *hated* my body, I was ashamed. I remember my attitude being an eye roll, and "Oh crap." I was little in stature, and my body was turning on me. The bullying from 4th grade had stopped, but now *this*. My attitude never improved about my periods. They were painful and messy, and I thought they smelled putrid.

  Kotex pads leaked like crazy. They ruined many of my pants and created embarrassing trips to the nurse's office in junior high school. My periods were ungodly painful, heavy and dismal. I felt like I squished when I walked, and the putrid smell. My mom took me to a gynecologist, and I got a pap smear at 11. (*Horrors*! Oh, fucking gawd, who would do that to a small girl. I looked about 8. Except for the Kotex protruding from my butt, I could easily pass for it.) I dreaded my periods. Birth control pills would've sufficed the problem at 12, but the year was around 1973. It was unheard of, even sinful, to put a child on birth control pills even for menstrual disorders. Each monthly period left me feeling depressed, irritable, and sick.

Mom's gynecologist was a weird-shaped man with grey hair and wired rimmed glasses and had a nasal tone when he spoke. Apparently, he was also *her* mom's gynecologist. I thought he was strange. His hands were huge with thick fingers, broader than my 11-year-old vaginal opening. He had me place my little legs in the stirrups I barely reached, after I disrobed and slipped on a revealing hospital gown that went around me twice. I could barely adjust my bare butt on the table, and the pillow seemed miles from my head. The gynecologist did the most agonizing pap smear and left the room while I dressed. I was given a THICK maternal pad in case I bled. (Good lord do I have to bleed anymore?) I don't remember there being a lab test for iron but should've been, considering the blood loss.

The gynecologist prescribed Darvocet. When my next period started, squirming and crying from the abdominal cramps, dreary from depression, I took one. Darvocet made me so sick that I was off school for a week writhing in nausea and vomiting pink pill coating. My breasts hurt; my body was fighting back. Every month I missed a week of school. Darvocet did no good at all, in fact, made me worse so I stopped taking them.

Nothing helped my moods, which I kept private, and pretended I was fine. This was to be a growing pattern.

Once my mom and I were grocery shopping, and I found a bottle Midol on the shelves. I slipped a bottle in the cart. The next month when my symptoms started, I took two Midol tablets. (I learned to feel symptoms a little before my period started, but there never was much of a warning of the embarrassing, ghastly bloody explosion in my pants.) The Midol tablets had a way of curbing the pain, and the bloating. I had my mom buy some Excedrin, and that helped the headache. Without the bloating, pain and headache, I could get through the period week just barely.

I had menstruation accidents in junior high school that were so embarrassing I wanted to die. When I had a period accident in school, I tried to get to the nurse's office before anyone saw blood seeping out of the crotch of my jeans. My period literally snuck up on me, and even tracking the date was no help. Menstrual accidents became a repulsive way of life.

One bloody accident in 8th grade, I was wearing peach-colored jeans. Blood started seeping out of my crotch, and the entire backside was red. I had to put my butt against the school wall and hide my backside until I got to the nurse's office. The nurse couldn't reach my mom and had to take me home to change.

Chapter 8

SEVENTH GRADE-IT'S YOUR PROBLEM, SO FACE IT

I attended one of the worst junior high schools in the state, Savannah Junior High School 1. There was a Savannah Junior High School 2 on the other side of the town closer to the farms. The students were frightening, uncaring, out for themselves. The students were "freaks" meaning druggies, or "Jocks" who were athletic. The students between the line of freaks and jocks were "boring." I was scared to death of both groups and considered "boring." I hated junior high school.

    Continuing in the orchestra in seventh grade, I carried my violin in its case two days a week on the bus.

I rode a bus that picked me up across the street from my house. The bullying started when one of the girls on the bus took my violin from beneath my seat and began to hand it up over her head to the person sitting behind.

"*What is wrong with me? I didn't ask for this,*" I thought. My self-esteem, shy and scared of the students, sunk even lower. Every student on the bus pointed at me, and then passed the violin back to my seat. It happened numerous times. I never said anything. I was afraid of the students and couldn't approach the bus driver. In the past if I said anything, the bullying became worse.

Regarding this situation, I can give credit to one of the substitute bus drivers. He saw the laughter and commotion of my violin being passed to the front of the bus, He pulled the bus to the side of the road and yelled,

"What the hell is going on?"

Someone laughed, pointed at me and said, "dummy violin girl."

The bus driver yelled, "Who's violin is this?"

I rose my hand and feebly said, "Mine."

He said, "You people better give her back her violin, if I ever see this crap anymore, every one of you damn people will be barred from ever riding this goddamned bus. You hear me? That shit is going to stop." The students went silent.

My violin was returned, and the bullying on the bus stopped if the substitute was driving. The thing is, the substitute bus driver pointed me out to the students, they got mad, and began picking on me even more inside the school.

In art class, I learned to paint on canvas. I enjoyed art class except I never was able to draw like I wanted to. In my mind, I had aspirations of being an artist and attending the Art Institute in Maryville, or even better, the Art Institute of Kansas City. The paint seemed messy, but I loved the feel of the canvas and the freedom of the brush. I found different paint brushes had different jobs and different canvasses or paper provided different textures. If I had pursued my interest in painting, I wonder if I'd be in a gallery? To my 7th grade mind, people who had artwork placed in galleries were the ultimate success.

The art teacher assigned everyone in my class to paint a self-portrait, telling us, "You only get one canvas. Make this one good." Someone walked by me and threw blue paint on my clothes and the picture. I had worked hard the entire class period to paint my portrait. The cruel and demeaning experience made it difficult not to mention embarrassing, to turn the portrait in at the end of class, so I didn't.

The art teacher saw my painting and said, "This is not going to get you a good grade. You weren't supposed to smear the paint. What are you, five?"

This time I quietly said, "Someone spilled blue paint on me, and it got on my pink windbreaker. I think they threw it on me."

The art teacher rolled her eyes.

I wore the blue paint on my windbreaker for the rest of the day. I never even got acknowledged or given a chance to repaint for the ruined portrait. It was the ultimate shame. I didn't forgive that person because total forgiveness isn't a life requirement. That's okay, I personally think all this humility built up to something larger I couldn't control after high school. Maybe that was part of my cause and effect, but it was karma that I didn't cause.

I *detested* gym class. My arms and legs couldn't jump correctly or perform how the teacher expected. I probably still needed to go to RC, but my sessions had stopped. My gym teacher, Mrs. Banks had strong legs and biceps and a short manly haircut and liked to single me out in class saying how "Rhonda isn't throwing the ball correctly. No wonder you never get chosen for class teams," with her loud manly voice. I had gym class on Tuesdays and Thursdays. We would sit in a row along the gym floor. Mrs. Banks had her favorites, she hated me.

For students labeled "boring," gym consisted mostly of government testing and preparing for governmental testing. Jocks got the privilege of football practice. Freaks did whatever they wanted. Class control didn't exist. If I had to perform the high jump for the government test, I always jumped crooked. And it's funny how I remember the government testing. It grated my nerves when Mrs. Banks focused on government requirements. "This week is the government phys-ed testing." (Lyndon B. Johnson started this thing of *government testing*, and to me, he could stuff it up his ass.) Half the time I didn't want to try. Why bother? Mrs. Banks pointed at me when I failed, which was most of the time. The class laughed, except for a couple of people.

My arm couldn't use a baseball bat. And when teams chose captains? I was the last person standing, waiting to be considered on whichever side, "Which team gets the failure?", I heard the student's mumble. The students who were already on a team pointed to me. As the usual teacher response, Mrs. Banks shrugged her shoulders and tended to her athletic favorites.

Then to top that off girls had to take showers naked together in junior high. It totally immobilized me, and I'm sure it debilitated other girls. Part of the dilemma with girls today could be related to body image comparing themselves with other girls in the school gym locker room. It's not a shower, *it's a display rack.* Girls weren't used to being naked in the shower in front of other girls unless they played on a sports team.

General whispers and gross observations included: "Her stomach is so flat, look at her ribs."

"What? She *shaves* it. Her boyfriend put her up to it. I think he likes it that way."

"I thought she stuffed her bra; no *way* is she that big."

"She needs to start shaving her legs, she looks like a gorilla."

"I thought she was fatter than that."

"Her tampon string is showing."

Once in the class right after gym, a guy whispered to me, "Does she have a pretty pussy?" I almost barfed from the disgust.

Showering is meant to get rid of sweat, so you don't offend other class members. Showering naked in front of other naked girls, in the locker room, in a class, as opposed to a team situation was exasperating. The thought, to me, "this is gross." Maybe I took it too seriously. I've never talked to other women to see how they felt at that age, showering together. Maybe I'm the minority thinking.

I tried to shower in the group with a towel covering my private parts, which I hated anyway. Pubic hair was disgusting and mine was dark brown. Other girls did the same. There had to be a better way. A lot of us made up excuses but found out we couldn't have a menstrual cycle three weeks out of the month, though mine felt that way. Mrs. Banks didn't believe us that we even had periods. Sponge baths would be a much better solution, with a few private showers. I don't know what kind of person thought to group young girls together in a large open shower room. I hope I never have to repeat that horrible experience. Granted, it wasn't as bad as in the book Carrie by Stephen King that I read later in the year. At least no one threw tampons at each other, that I know of.

During junior high, I played violin in the orchestra. The junior high orchestra was not for the popular kids, it was for the boring kids. Music class lacked sustenance, and I'm surprised I continued to excel. The teacher, Mr. Wallace, was the band instructor. There was no theory or technique. The orchestra in junior high was for losers and non-achievers.

I loved English, art, and choir. Outside of school I still danced and took private violin and piano classes. In choir, I wanted to excel. I strived for this all through junior high and in high school. I loved choir but didn't reach the success I needed. Aiming for something you never succeed is exhausting and rigorous. I thought the choir sounded pretty and did fun activities. I was well aware of the work they put in for that type of success. The choir in both junior high and high school was one of the most successful programs in the state. I was willing to practice and do what was involved. There were numerous auditions, and I never gave up trying. In high school, I succeeded in being accepted in the choir for only one year. I took glee club because I wanted to sing. The auditioning for both junior high and high school glee club only existed to find out what part you sang. It was exciting after auditions to see my name on the list of Glee Club. I wanted so bad to have a role in the smaller singing groups in both junior high and high school. It never happened.

At home, I remember my dad cussing at Nixon, "Goddamned Republican. He's a crook," when the president spoke on our little color television, while we ate dinner together as a family, which was often. Family politics were a huge matter at our house. My dad bought a color TV as soon as they were available. The football team was red and white, and the movies had green grass and blue skies.

I spent afternoons reading books beyond my age or swinging on my swing in the backyard when I wasn't practicing violin. I started to detest the word "practice." It sounded raspy and forced. I played fetch with Pete, and always did my homework. I didn't have many friends and didn't like anyone at the school. I tried to be social, as best I could.

My weekend activities were hiking and walking with my mom. Savannah had beautiful scenery and walking trails. Sometimes my mom and I would hike on the trails together on Saturdays, pausing to see a goose or duck near the Andrew County Museum grounds. It was a nice get-away from the horrors of junior high.

Savannah Junior High School 1 had a football and basketball team. I joined the pep club. I tried out for the marching corps but didn't make the cut. While eavesdropping, the cheerleaders whispered something critical about my "thighs." "Her thighs are too large to look attractive in the short skirts." (Echo that same phrase in high school and college. *Lady Ana* seemed to be selecting me for grooming). I doubt that I could've marched in time, so they probably did me a favor. I took the thigh comment very seriously and started doing leg lifts and plies at home in my room with the door closed. In gym (Mrs. Banks class), we learned how to "exercise those fat abs, girls." (I always thought she was looking at me.) At the time, I could only do 25 crunches at once. I worked the crunches in with the plies in my room at home with the door closed. (Secrecy is one of Lady Anna's skills.)

In pep club, we wore black skirts and a green school t-shirt. The black skirts were required to be an inch above our kneecap. My mom hemmed my skirt. I wore it to school on football days. I noticed the popular girl's skirts were much shorter. I went home and told my mom about the girl's skirts that were too short. There wasn't much we could do, but I noticed it at every game.

Chapter 9

DISCALULA IS A MONSTER

I couldn't have been worse in math and might've been diagnosed as having "Discalcula-mild," as in the DSMIV. In eighth grade, I was placed in "Basics Math." Held in a small room, one of the special-ed teachers taught the Basic Math class. The special-ed class was adjacent, through a door in the back of the room. The people in the Basics Math class didn't even know how to add. Everyone in the school knew I attended *Basic Math*. On rare occasions, one of the special-ed kids wandered into the Basic Math class and had to be redirected back into her room, amidst derogatory comments from the boys in Basic Math. If the teacher let the door open to the special -d class, the boys in Basic Math mocked the kids.

I never knew if the special-ed kids were autistic, had Downs or were mentally or physically disabled. There was a mixture of kids with different development or mental disorders. The special-ed class had at least 25 students in the large room. It was kept dark. It wasn't a good set up to have the Basic Math class door lead into the special-ed class.

Infrequent smells of uncontrolled bodily functions wafted through the open door, and the teacher was exasperated, especially if the second special-ed teacher was out sick.

The Basic Math teacher often went into the special-ed room to help "clean" one of the students. "I'll help you clean her up. Did she have an accident?" She asked the second special-ed teacher. "Yes, Mary pooped again, in her pants!" yelled the special-ed teacher. I wanted to hide in embarrassment, but really felt nothing for Mary. Pooping in pants was an embarrassing subject.

When the teacher left the room one of the guys in class would talk at length about "which retard pooped their pants? It was Mary." I went home that day and told my parents that "Mary pooped her pants in the Special-Ed class." My mom corrected me and said, "You're not supposed to talk about who popped their pants at school."

The students in Basic Math were the type who lit up cigarettes the minute the teacher left the room. The students in Basic Math passed baggies of marijuana, and Ritalin to each other when the teacher was *in* the room.

The Basic Math students used curse words at will. The students said, "fuck this", when the teacher explained math equations, loud enough for the teacher to hear. I don't even remember having homework. I only remember trying to figure out how to be invisible. The students were scary. But I endured the class and learned skills that didn't include math.

The ninth graders liked to block the eighth and seventh graders in the hallway making them late to class, often lining themselves in the hallway so the younger students couldn't walk through the halls. This happened a lot. I also got my books dumped about once a week, another regular day in junior high.

I saw kids pick the locks of hall lockers. I never had my locker broken into while in school. Nor did I see a teacher try to stop any of the bullying even though they saw what took place.

      After school, I attended junior varsity football or basketball games, pep rallies, did homework, had sleepovers when I didn't have dance nights. Eventually having to phase out something and decided on dance class. I became too busy with extracurricular activities. When by myself, I wrote poetry, journals and listened to the Rolling Stones, practiced violin and learned cross stitch. Sometimes I painted.

CHAPTER 10

GO ASK THE BULLIES, EVERYTHING'S FINE

Being bullied every day in seventh and eighth grade in junior high took a climatic toll. Though I've never been sexually abused or raped, after the act, women feel disjointed and withdrawn. CASA describes the feelings after the rape of "powerless and loss of control"; the feelings of "emotional numbness," "guilt and self-blame", "embarrassment", "mood changes." (secasa.com)

I turned to books and reading, as an escape. The junior high students frightened me, and rightly so. I started to feel powerless, loss of control, emotional numbness, guilt, self-blame, embarrassment.

During the day Savannah was beautiful, oak and elm trees green leaves shadowing over fields. The grass green, and air clean. With the outside beauty of nature, who could imagine my dark feelings that I carried in my head, unable to tell anyone?

One night at home alone, after being blocked in the hall, having my books dumped twice, getting my bra strap snapped, being humiliated for being a "dummy" in Basic Math, and getting my violin passed from the back of the bus to the front of the bus, I "cracked."

My thoughts turned dark and inward. I wanted an escape and books I read weren't helping. I couldn't approach a teacher, I was embarrassed, and if I tried, the students would find out and the bullying would become worse. On top of that, I hated approaching teachers or asking questions, and one on one counseling, no way could I tell them what was going on. I was stymied from telling the students to stop. School counselors were useless because if you were seen going to the counselor, you'd be teased the next morning. I wanted so bad to have good grades, but mine were dropping. I was pointed and singled out by the students, it seemed, every move I made was wrong.

My bullying began in phases. The first phase was verbal, teasing. The students called me names, "Rhonda Honda who sucks Hondas," after they saw my dad taking me to school on his new Honda motorcycle. They laughed at me, and every day they accused me of stuffing my bra. "You have toilet paper in your bra, why don't you take it out, flatsy?" I began to wear t-shirts that were a little larger than perfect fit. They snapped my bra strap, often pulling my hair which was beautiful, long, with waves.

They called me "elephant butt", because I had a big butt, despite ballet classes. They called me "violin shrill" (instead of girl) because I played the violin. They didn't tease anyone else in orchestra. They called me "chipmunk" because I had a round face. (Note to self: big butt, round face, extra fat). The only thing perfect with my body was my long hair which laid in ringlets almost down to my waist.

One particularly cruel prank the students played on me was an invitation to a cheerleader's birthday party. I couldn't believe I was going to Sharin's birthday party! I was so excited, and everything had to be perfect from the present, from the wrapping paper, to my clothes I wore. She lived a couple of blocks away and our moms bowled together. Sharin and I were indifferent to each other, and never spoke.

In my school locker, I found a birthday party invitation that someone dropped through the vents. It was an invitation to Sharin's birthday party the next Saturday. I brought it home, excited. My mom marked the date on the calendar, "Birthday party" in red pen. Mom and I shopped for Sharin's present, a purse from Macy's. I bought a new outfit, and even did crunches to make sure my stomach was flat. I made up what I thought were Jazzercise routines for my "big butt" and started faithfully repeating them in front of the mirror in my room.

On the day written on the invitation, my mom drove me to Sharin's house. I had low heeled shoes, and my special outfit. My long hair was curled in brown spirals. I clutched the pretty wrapped package and knocked on her door. The house was huge but looked oddly vacant like no one was home.

I had the invitation in my purse, and double checked the time. I arrived a few minutes early. My mom sat outside in the car, and I kept knocking at the door. No one answered. Wasn't she home? Maybe they were around the back? I went to the back, but no one was in the yard. No one was home. I dreaded telling my mom. We both decided the invitation was written with the wrong date. Once we were home, I unwrapped the gift, my mom replaced the price tags, and returned the purse.

On Monday in every single class, someone said, "Did you enjoy the party? How was it? Was the cake good?" I frowned and looked away. I started to lose hope. When I saw Sharin in the hall, I was unable to approach her to ask her why she would do such a thing. I did nothing to her to make her mad. I went home and told my mom that I didn't do a thing to Sharin. My mom talked to her mom, and I noticed she bowled with someone different after the party incident.

During the teasing phase of the bullying, I would go home, and read. Books like *Go Ask Alice* and *Are You There God, It's Me, Margaret*, were in the public library. The library was within walking distance from my house. I spent a lot of Saturdays pondering over the many books. I read one or more books a week. One of the books that I'm kind of surprised I didn't read was "*Catcher in the Rye.*" by J D Salinger. I finally read it in 2016.

My periods in seventh and eighth grade were explosive, painful and unpredictable and depressive. After the period accident with the peach jeans, I heard whispers for two weeks. "She started her period, and it got all over her pants. She is so gross, and she smells." I thought I had hidden my bloody jeans from everyone. It wouldn't surprise me if the school nurse told one of the parents and the word got out.

I learned to alleviate period incidents by always carrying pads and tampons and wearing tunic tops. My mom didn't allow tampons, but I was able to buy them with my allowance during walks around Savannah. If I wore tampons, I had to double them up with a thick pad that showed under my jeans. My periods were out of control, making me hate my body even more. After Midol, at least symptoms were kind of controlled. The uterine bleeding was not. Along with the teasing about my big butt, this began what accumulated as a disastrous outcome and ruined self-esteem. My depression sank lower, but I hid it well.

Phase 2 of the bullying was physical. Every move I made was noticed, measured and evaluated with verbal ridicule. My thoughts grew darker. Once the teasing became physical (dumping my books, blocking me in halls, pulling my ponytail, snapping my bra), I felt like I wanted to step outside my body. I wanted to disappear. Once I got tripped in class, broke my foot and was on crutches, but I got out of school for a while. I had to do my schoolwork at home, quiet and relieved for a moment.

One night I'd had enough bullying. I was 15 (10th grade), my periods left me drained, depressed and I wanted to die. I found a razor, a poorly selected razor at that. I wasn't planning on cutting myself or scratching or doing anything self-destructive. It just happened. I went into the private bathroom that no one used. I sat in the vanity chair. I cut my wrist.

The blood scared me, and I cleaned up and no one knew any different. Unfortunately, everything was fine.

The razor sort of dug deep into my wrist which was tiny and thin. As I cut deeper, I felt the sharp blade dig into my epidermis, then my dermis and skin layers below. Fearful of cutting deeper and frankly not wanting a bloodier scene, I stopped. It was painfully numb. That's the only way of describing the feeling after cutting. I cut so deep on my wrist; it made a one-inch permanent scar that I can still see. It became a weird habit. Every time I scratched or cut; I stopped before I reached blood.

After cutting my wrist, I got smart thinking people would see the scars, and I started cutting my foot where no one would ever notice. I didn't cut every night, only when my emotions cracked. In one setting, I pricked dots on the instep for my left inner foot. The dots I created remind me now of a tattoo I saw on Google recently that read:

"------Cut on thin line------"

How appropriate.

I read the book *Go Ask Alice* at least three times in eighth grade. In the book, she carves "Alice" on her arm. I'd never go that far. In fact, even at 13, when I read the book, I thought, "If you had cut your foot, no one would've seen the scar." Where did that thought originate? I have no idea how I learned cutting; I didn't learn from a book. I would guess *Go Ask Alice* made a difference in my life, but so did *On The Road* when I read it at 16. *Go Ask Alice* opened a path to other self-destructive behaviors in later adolescence.

Chapter 11

NINTH GRADE

The teasing and bullying stopped in ninth grade. Just as the seasons in Savannah were remarkably different in colors and smells in the air, the climate in the classroom changed.

I was traumatized from seventh and eighth grade. Of course, I never joined the group of ninth grade students dumping books or blocking the halls, heck I didn't join anything because I didn't like the other students. But at last, no one picked on me. I was a ninth grader, and I was supposed to be proud. The teachers expected ninth graders to be leaders. I wasn't a leader; I was a dud.

With a better attitude, my grades improved. While Orchestra was dull and lame, I enjoyed my Typing class, Choir and English Composition. I also loved my science class. My instructor was phenomenal. Her name was Mrs. Clanders. Her husband also taught and was as well liked as she. She had long brown spiraled hair that she often pulled back into a long ponytail. She wore pants or jeans and cute blouses. What I really liked about her appearance was her perfect make up. Her personality was cheery and upbeat. I had good grades in Science and Mrs. Clanders talked me into joining the Science Club.

The Science Club traveled to Chicago to see the Museum of Science and Industry in the spring. The Fairy Castle exhibit was spectacular. The castle was a miniature scale replica that even had electricity. It had a miniature fairy garden and miniature fairies. In another room of the museum, there was a miniature White House complete with an oval office and Christmas tree. I had never seen anything this beautiful. I was drawn to the lights and colors. This was the highlight of my entire nine years in school. When ninth graded ended, I crossed my fingers looking forward to high school.

    The summer of my ninth-grade year, I spent swinging on my monkey swing attached to the oak tree in the back yard or running in Savannah City Park. I looked about 12. I thought I could run and maybe be in a race one day. Savannah had miles of dense wooded areas, never called forests. People who lived there simply called the area, "the woods." In convenience stores, and gas stations, there was always a story amongst residents of children getting lost in the woods of Savannah. "Boy, something must've got her. There must be something in those woods." I knew enough not to run in the woods. I was afraid of who might be hiding.

Chapter 12

DRIVING ME CRAZY

I turned sixteen in 10th grade and prepared to take my driver's license test. I passed the written but froze from nerves during the driving part of the exam. It was difficult for me to physically show someone how to do something that required demonstration. That included the driving test.

During the first semester of 10th grade, I took Driver's Ed. I was sick when they taught parallel parking and missed that portion of class. I knew how to drive, but I repeatedly flunked the driving portion. One of my six tries the examiner didn't like how I held the steering wheel and flunked me. How *absurd*! I had the same examiner three separate times. Each time I had him I rolled my eyes, "You've got to be kidding."

I finally got my first driving license in May of 1978 with a different instructor. The family celebrated with pizza in a buffet near Savannah Square.

I developed weird driving OCD habits. I had to check my purse 3 times to make sure I had my keys, which is a good habit but a bit obsessive. I made car rules. No one could eat in my car. No trash in my car. I still hate parking lots because that's where people get careless and hit other cars accidently. I have gotten over the fear of being hit in a parking lot. I still check for my keys in my purse several times before I lock the door. I have no idea how people parallel park, personally it scares me.

Chapter 13

TENTH GRADE, JAMES DEAN AND LESTER

My tenth-grade year 15-16 years old, I studied music theory, choir, violin, but no sports. My gym class was a 1st Year Dance. I played first chair violin and soloed during the high school musical Oklahoma. I had three of the best teachers in the high school: Choir, English teacher and Communications teacher. As a reminder, I only succeeded one year to be accepted in the actual choir. My periods became progressively worse. I did the wrist cutting incident during this time, that no one knew about and could've killed me had I not gotten scared of my own blood, which I saw a lot of every month.

Sixteen is often when "*ED*" (eating disorder) introduces itself to teenagers susceptible to his affliction. (ncbi, 2004) I had no idea of "*Ed*", or even problems with food whatsoever except for a fascination with calories. A rumor spread about one of the cheerleaders who started dieting and couldn't stop. How could she do *that*? I kept trying to mentally picture her *that* skinny. She was an urban legend.

At the first football game in tenth grade there were 12 cheer leaders. At the last basketball game later in the year, there were 11. I realized the students told the truth.

In tenth grade I learned the cheerleader who wasn't in class ate two meals a day, then dropped to one.

Her sister caught her vomiting in the bathroom and told their mother.

"But I vomited a few weeks ago with the stomach flu," I told my friend, Portia.

"Girl," she said at lunch, "Don't you realize what I mean?" She demonstrated by putting her finger to her mouth. I had developed a few friends who weren't lifelong. Portia was a black girl in many of my classes and we sat together at lunch. She had a large frame and short brown hair.

"Oh," I stood silent in deep thought. Hmm. "Maybe that will work for my last ten pounds," I said.

Portia said "Girl, it might work for my 30."

Our dog, Pete, was getting old, and eventually got hip dysplasia. We had to put him to sleep. I cried for days. Pete was my best friend. The house was empty, sad and quiet without a dog. About a month later, my dad surprised me and bought home a west highland terroir named Snowball.

I saw *Rebel Without a Cause* when I was 16 and I loved James Dean. I idolized Natalie Woods. Natalie Woods was the co-essential teenage girl, after all she hung out with James Dean. Her body was perfectly proportioned to her waist and her hair and face was perfect. I wanted to be her. I watched *Rebel Without a Cause* as often as I could.

In 1978, McDonalds served ice cream as a test product in Maryville, MO. It tasted grand. Oh, the sweetness and creamy goodness about to be consumed by my mouth. I drove my mom's car to school, always carefully checking for my keys three times when locking the door and parking. When driving home from high school I made regular stops at McDonalds often for ice cream and a plain cheeseburger. Occasionally I left McDonalds coughing, reaching for my inhaler because of my milk allergy.

    I was a picky eater, making demands this way and that. Cheeseburgers and sandwiches ordered plain, no food touching, unless it's Chinese. No steak ever was on my plate or in my mouth, and if mustard was anywhere near my sandwich, I sent the food back. Mexican was my favorite food, but I was picky about what I ordered. With the plain cheeseburger issue, I was kind of a drag to eat with at McDonald's. I was the one everyone had to wait for, and sometimes it took a long time to get my food.

The first night I watched *Rebel Without a Cause*, I drove to McDonalds for ice cream and a plain cheeseburger. They were slow in making my ice cream cone. I got home in time to see the very beginning of the movie. James Dean sat on a chair in juvenile hall, found Natalie Wood's mirrored compact that she dropped on the floor while Sal Mineo was in trouble in the next room for abusing puppies.

James Dean had the perfect charm. Lost and edgy, but tender. I bought a red jacket exactly like James Dean and wore it everywhere. I kept looking for my own James Dean, but I didn't have enough popularity at school to date any guy who even resembled him, so I gave up that goal and changed my standards. The guys I had my eyes on ended up being jerks. One got arrested 20 years later for spouse abuse.

In high school Communications class, the teacher whose name resembled a Grateful Dead member, Mr. Lesk, wrote "F U C K" in chalk on the chalk board one letter at a time, erasing each letter before writing the next. "If I write it on the board, you won't be shocked when I say it, nor will you go home and tell your parents who might be doing it right now."

I learned about Buddhism and meditation from Mr. Lesk. He was cool. He described himself as a Buddhist and a Deadhead. I thought how fortunate I am to have him for an instructor. I learned later he moved to Tibet to become a Buddhist monk. I learned basic meditation in Communications class. He led guided meditations daily. Our homework consisted of recorded guided meditations that we did outside while walking and quiet dark black mediation and guided meditation in our bedroom. The beautiful trees and grassland in Savannah made the perfect backdrop for my walking meditation homework. Meditation tried to quiet my mind. Ana tried to poison it.

    Mr. Lesk mentioned the Beat Generation, Jack Kerouac, and Neal Cassady. We read poems by Allen Ginsberg, then meditated for a half an hour. I learned how to ground myself through meditation and how to flow my energy. We played with energy balls, and he showed us crystals from Arkansas. Occasionally, he'd bring his tarot cards to class and teach us a little about the tarot. He often did intuitive readings for us, using palmistry, tarot cards or I-ching. Then I'd go home and do my meditation homework. Again, I need to reiterate, the class was called "Communications."

After I got my driver's license, my dad bought me a brown Pacer. Glass encasement if I remember right. I drove to a local bookstore in Savannah and *On the Road* by Jack Kerouac fell on my foot out of nowhere from a full shelf of books about marine life and nature. I bought the book along with the *DhamaPada* and read both. I was 16. From the same bookstore I bought the Diamond Sutra and Heart Sutra and later almost every book Jack Kerouac wrote.

During high school, there was a boy lurking around me named Lester. He looked like a cowboy but liked rock music. He wore plaid button-down shirts over white t-shirts, slightly acid washed jeans and cowboy boots. Every guy in Savannah wore cowboy boots, as did most of us girls. He looked like he should have a cowboy hat on as well. He had dark brown short hair, and brown dreamy eyes. He didn't play sports, but he had muscles. He was a handsome cowboy. I decided when I saw him that he would be my boyfriend. I had an instant crush.

I couldn't approach him because I was too shy. He followed me to orchestra. "I wanted to see what instrument you played." How odd, I thought.

At lunch time in the cafeteria, he asked to sit across from me on the bench. We talked about our classes. We were in a couple of classes together, and he started sitting next to me. One day he passed me a note when the teacher wasn't looking. It said, "Meet me at KFC after school." I looked at him, smiled and nodded.

Kentucky Fried Chicken was adjacent to the high school. I walked to the restaurant and saw Lester sitting at a booth. I said, "Hi," and waved. We frequently met at Kentucky Fried Chicken. Our conversations grew deeper. In the school cafeteria our conversations didn't seem to matter. I showed him the Diamond Sutra and he showed me the current issue of Old Farmer's Almanac. He borrowed the Diamond Sutra from me. I borrowed Old Farmer's Almanac from him.

Chapter 14

THE FARM

Lester always wore a brown Carhartt; not anything close to the jacket James Dean wore in *Rebel Without a Cause*. I always pictured myself with a boy wearing a James Dean jacket, and certainly not the common cowboy boots. Lester was disciplined and clean, certainly not a bad boy. Lester had the utmost polite manners. If I was cold, he let me wear his jacket, which smelled like mowed grass. I had my cowboy and he made me happy, and he even smelled like a farm boy!

Within two months of meeting at Kentucky Fried Chicken, he invited me to go to his farm in Eastern Savannah. He picked me up at home, met my parents and seemed comfortable. My mom remarked how handsome he looked. He drove his dad's truck, an old grey Ford. He was always well groomed and smelled like Old Spice and mowed grass. Lester's smile made him look boyish. He was genuinely mannerly to my mom. Once when picking me up he bought my mom a bouquet of flowers picked from his dad's garden.

    I was a fan of John Steinbeck and had read and seen the movie East *of Eden*. I even had the sheet music to the theme of *East of Eden* and could partially play it on the piano. I saw *East of Eden* every time it was on TV. Lester's giant farm looked like the fields described in *East of Eden*. I remember the first time I saw the green pasture hills of Lester's farm. The colors spanned all hues of green. The air was fresh with whiffs of grass, trees, and a few cows.

Savannah was surrounded by grassland. Lester's family lived on a vast farm. Lester's dad, Joe, owned a large portion of the land in Eastern Savannah. It included acres of open fields with cows grazing, chickens and pigs, a few goats and a large vegetable garden. Lester's dad sold his vegetables through his own company at Savannah City Market. He also delivered vegetables to restaurants in Maryville in his company truck. But his main company business was milk.

Lester had a younger brother whose name was Cooper. He was eight. He'd follow his brother when we went into the pig shed or chicken coop. Cooper helped milk the goats and the cows. When we went to the vegetable garden, little Cooper followed, picking tomatoes.

"Mom will like these, won't she, Les?"

"She sure will, Cooper."

Lester's mom, Mary, loved to make pies. With each visit, there were pies in the window- sill, just like photograph of a farmhouse. The pies were always delicious prompting me to ask, "What's your secret?"

"Sugar in the crust, and real butter instead of Crisco. You can never go wrong if you use those 2 ingredients. And over fill pies with filling," said Mary. She wore a kitchen apron over her clothes.

Many evenings, I'd end up at Lester's for dinner. Lester's dad, Joe had bought the neighbor's farm and planned on buying more dairy cows.

"All my cows out there are dairy cows. We have one bull. He stays busy," said Joe.

He was in the process of branding his milk, calling it Les and Cooper.

"We experiment with flavors. You like banana milk?"

"I'm allergic to milk." I answered. "But I'll try it."

"Hold up now, Lester, did you know she was allergic to milk?" asked his dad in a country drawl and a condescending glance.

"Yeah dad, but..." Lester looked at me with such cute ornery smile.

I drank a big gulp. Whew, it was a close call because I avoided any type of milk for over 12 years. It was sweet and unlike any milk I'd ever imagine. It magically went down my throat without a cough.

Later that evening, Joe showed me the bottles he was planning on using for Les and Cooper Milk. "I've perfected banana milk, peach, chocolate, strawberry. The only flavor I can't figure out how to perfectly concoct is vanilla flavored milk."

"Are you going to be a milk man?" I asked.

"We're going to sell our milk in every store in the region. Would you like to help me hand out samples at country stores around here?" Joe asked.

"I would," I said.

It was time to leave, and I couldn't wait to tell my mom I drank milk and didn't barf.

Lester and I enjoyed frolicking in the field, as long as we could ditch Cooper. Cooper was sweet and I didn't mind him being around. Lester liked to chase Cooper into the garden and then pretend he couldn't see him. Cooper *was* short and we couldn't see him standing under the corn stalks. But Cooper really thought he was lost. It was painfully funny. When we saw Cooper running away, Lester would sneak a kiss on my cheek. He had the softest lips, and that smell again. I figured out that smell. It wasn't Old Spice, Teen Spirit, or freshly mowed grass, but hay bales. I could always tell if he'd mowed the lawn or helped bale hay.

In the late winter through spring, he wore a brown Carhartt coat. I always thought Carhartt's were sexy on boys. For my 17th birthday, he gave me a Carhartt coat. The only colors available in 1979 were basic brown, black and grey. Grey was hard to find. Grey, being my favorite color, I mentioned to him, "I always wanted a grey Carhartt."

On my 17th birthday, Lester knocked on the door with a large package wrapped meticulously in birthday paper. I was practicing violin for a spring concert. Lester was waiting on me in the living room. My mom and dad were there, talking. I opened the large box, and inside was a beautiful grey Carhartt coat. I squealed with delight and threw my arms around him. We had pepperoni pizza and birthday cake. Lester said, "My dad should've bought the ice cream." Of course, there was no ice cream at the table with my milk allergy. Lester's dad's ice cream was the only kind I could eat without having a coughing fit. My mom and dad gave me a silver ID bracelet with a heart charm. ID bracelets were all the rage. I wore it and the Carhartt every day.

Chapter 15

ELEVENTH GRADE

Eleventh grade was full of music contests and auditions. I told my parents I was going to major in music and be a music therapist at Northwest Missouri State University in Maryville, or maybe in Warrensburg at CMSU. I spent hours practicing violin for my college audition.

In eleventh grade, I befriended students older than I; some of whom are still my friends. Jeremy and Michael both played in orchestra. Jeremy ended up being one of my best friends.

I learned to wear long sweaters for my monthly visitor and borrowed tampons unbeknownst to my mom. (She STILL didn't like me to wear tampons). And I bought them, secretly. I subsided the pain with Midol. If I complained of pain, I was taken to the gynecologist who stuffed me with Darvocet, which I already knew, made me sick. I flushed them down the toilet. I stopped complaining. My mood was dismal and dull.

Seventeen was a great year. In the spring when Lester and I had more time together, we became close. I was terrified. When the magic began to happen between us, I thought I would get pregnant by just looking at a penis. The idea was crazy seeming we hadn't even kissed. I knew about sex education, but the thought of a penis scared the shit out of me.

One spring day Lester and I kissed on the lips behind a corn stalk in his dad's vegetable garden. Then we raced each other through the pasture, to the old barn. In the barn was filled with hay and cow feed. Lester smelled like mowed grass. I chased Lester up a rickety wooden ladder to the balcony. We fell in a pile of hay together. I kept thinking about the mighty frightful penis, "Oh my God, I'm going to get pregnant like Samantha in school did last year, shit," I thought.

Things got hot between us fast. In April 1979, at 17, I lost my virginity in the barn at Lester's dad's farm in the hay. I was nervous and excited and even scared of the dreaded penis. Lester pulled a condom out of his pants pocket. I didn't get pregnant looking at his penis, nor did I get pregnant using a condom. I did have to pull hay out of my butt.

The next morning, my vagina was sore, and I thought I walked funny. When I played my violin, it hurt to sit in certain positions and to I had to adjusting my butt. I didn't tell my mom. It kind of hurt when I peed, so I drank a gallon of water to pee some more. Being responsible, I decided I needed some type of birth control.

The following Monday I drove to Planned Parenthood in Maryville to get birth control pills. I used Planned Parenthood for a few years. I preferred them to a gynecologist, for my yearly pap smear. I hated going to the gynecologist. Mom's gynecologist still freaked me out.

Planned Parenthood in Maryville was comfortable, and I liked the nurse practitioners. They were female. It was a little office near a pizza place. The building looked plain, nondescript and not elegant.

In Maryville they allowed 17-year-old girls to obtain birth control pills without the parent's permission.

I looked young. The nurse said, "Are you sure you're 17? You look eleven."

The examination room was painted dull green with an examination table and stirrups. On the wall was a pictured diagram of a vagina and on the shelf was a plastic replica of a breast. The female nurse practitioner checked my urine for pregnancy. I complained about burning when I peed, so she checked my urine for bacteria. She gave me three months of birth control pills, and antibiotics for a urinary tract infection. She also warned me about smoking and using the pill, and high school drinking. I was afraid of smoking because I believed I'd get lung cancer and afraid of drinking because I might get drunk. My birth control pills cost $5.00. I drove home and began to take them as I was directed. I hid them in my sock drawer and didn't tell my mom about the antibiotics.

Almost a month later in the morning, I started throwing up. I was taking the pink placebo pills in the birth control package. I got violently ill. I had gained five pounds and was mortified. I traced it back to the birth control pills. My mom called the school thinking I had the stomach flu. I was sick for a couple of days. I called the nurse at Planned Parenthood who confirmed, "Some girls throw up while on the pill. Come in and we'll change the prescription." No easy feat. I had to figure out a reason to drive my car to Maryville while I was home sick barfing. When I was feeling better and able to drive, I told my mom I was going to the bookstore, "Oh, that's in Maryville, do you need it for English?"

"Yeah." I lied. She gave me a twenty. I drove back to Planned Parenthood and got a different prescription. I stopped at the bookstore, and bought a book, to make my mom happy and presented her with change.

I hadn't talked much to Lester while I was sick. He called and asked if everything was okay, and I told him my problem.

And of course, one out of four times (and it didn't matter if we were in Lester's room or in the hay), I ended up with a urinary tract infection and back to Planned Parenthood for antibiotics.

I never told my mom about the urinary tract infections, but always made sure she bought cranberry juice at the grocery store. My mom said, "You sure like cranberry juice."

I answered, "It's loaded with vitamin C. I learned that from Lester's dad."

Chapter 16

MUSICAL INTERLUDE

I practiced my violin for the high school orchestra Easter concert. The orchestra played the theme from Ten Commandments and the hymn, "Onward Christian Soldiers." The next week, I auditioned for the Northwest Missouri State University's orchestra and performed my musical placement exam for college. The placement exam was site reading a music piece and I passed. I was accepted for college as a music therapist major.

    I wasn't sure music therapy was what I wanted to do as a career. I questioned my choice. It was an up-and-coming occupation, but not hugely accepted.

As a career choice, music therapy was a complex move from my basic musician knowledge. It was too bold, and too mature. In the future, music therapy wasn't a popular choice.

For an up-and-coming career, in 2004, the job outlook of music therapist gradually failed as job demand increased. (CareersinPsychology.org) As a nurse, I've not seen successful music therapists. Most music therapists work on their own or are contracted, with little to no benefits. Some even take the path of freelancing.

I didn't realize in 1979 that the work would include weekend, weeknights, and would take at least four years to be certified. If I had thought, or had the ability to research the occupation, I would've come to a screeching halt before disaster.

Chapter 17

SUMMER OF '79

Summer of my junior year with Lester was full of love and flowers, cows and goats, ice cream and flavored milk. Lester's dad hired me to hand out milk samples at Class-Act Foods in Hamilton, MO, saying 'We need a pretty girl's face." Hamilton in 1979, had a total of 1,039 population with a few antique stores, one tractor shop, a gas station and Class-Act Foods. Hamilton was around 30 minutes from Savannah in 1979. It was a small country town.

    Lester's dad wanted to branch out the family business. What started in Savannah, grew to Hamilton, later I was handing out samples in St. Joseph, MO. I loved handing out samples. Everyone left happy, and most bought a bottle of milk. Lester's dad built a milk bottling factory near Savannah on a large acreage of land. His business model was "people paid a deposit when purchasing the bottles." When they returned the bottles, they received their deposit. Lester remained busy at the bottling factory.

Handing out tasty samples of banana and peach flavored milk at little country stores was great! I made fifty dollars for a few hours work every Saturday.

Some of the customers had never heard of banana or peach flavored milk, and it was well received. The stores made several orders, and Les and Cooper Milk started to be a success.

The success grew to butter, and later Les and Cooper Milk developed cheese. Lester's dad began to market their ice cream. They turned their dairy farm into a tourist attraction with a family day, allowing people to milk the dairy cow. They sold souvenirs that said Les and Cooper. Eventually they began to market their milk all the way to Kansas City, making Les and Cooper and well-known name.

Chapter 18

I WAS INCREDIBLY QUIET

Lester and I had a couple of classes together during our senior year. Everyone in school knew we dated. We spent hours discussing our future together. He was going to a different college in Utah, which is a long drive from Missouri. His college choice was important to him due to an agriculture degree that Maryville didn't offer. We decided to date long distance, with only phones or letters. But note, we had the rest of the year together.

The violin practicing got in the way of running, dancing, being active and my stomach and butt seemed to get larger than I wanted. Well, anything larger than a flat stomach didn't pass in my eyes. I had to have a flat stomach when I performed violin soloes and stood in front of orchestra. I started doing fifty crunches a day.

In the bathroom, in between classes, girls gathered and discussed how bad they hated their body parts: thighs, breasts, butts, gut. I hated my thighs, stomach and butt. After all, thighs and butt were the reason I didn't get selected for the marching corps in Savannah High School.

I tried out for the senior marching corps, practiced my solo march and knew my routine. Out of the mouth of the head cheerleader (the one who later starved herself) said to her friend, "Her thighs are too big." Wow. It echoed in my mind continuously through my senior year. I wanted to hide my huge thighs. It was a thought that rolled around in my head from *junior high*! I thought I had thunder thighs, and I wore a size nine jeans.

One girl who I thought was beautiful with perfect hair and make-up, and the newest purse, threatened to take a knife and cut her thighs one time in the girl's bathroom. At the school library, I began checking out every book I could about dieting and discovered every woman hates their thighs.

I hated my flabby gut, breasts, butt and round grapefruit shaped face. The whispered words from junior high resounded softly in my brain, "*Chipmunk*". It was an ongoing theme. I thought my stomach stuck out. My A-cup breasts were too big "*She stuffs her bra.*" My butt size made my jean size bigger than it should be when I passed a mirror. "*Elephant butt*". My round face reminded me of a cantaloupe. Granted, I wasn't very thin like the *popular* girls. And my butt was so huge, to me, it protruded in the hallway as I walked to classes. As a whole, the girls in high school didn't discuss their bodies except in the bathroom. In Gym no one talked to each other in the locker room. The girls hung out in the locker room to fix their make up at the mirror.

High school gym class was liberal about showering. However, I was able to avoid Gym for two years, taking dance classes. I still thought my thighs were huge. I made sure to keep my stomach flat for dance class and violin soloes, doing crunches and often eating 6 apples and that was all I ate for the day. I got away with it by telling my parents that I ate at KFC.

I bought Dexatrim diet pills and over the counter water pills one day at the drug store. I didn't need

Dexatrim, but I bought them. Lester found my Dexatrim sticking out of my purse and said, "Uh, you don't need these."

I was the smallest girl in my senior class, and the shortest. I made pretty good grades during my senior year and was in the pep club. I played violin in orchestra 1st or 2nd chair but envied the dancers. I thought I was too fat for dance.

I played the piano and seldom the guitar. My nails were too short, and I had to use a guitar pick. Lester and I attended music competitions in Warrensburg, (he didn't play any instruments), and I soloed on the violin. I got several score of 2's. I also got a couple of 1's.

Jeremy and Michael participated in music contest as college students, they graduated the year before. Jeremy played string bass and drums. Michael played piano. The three of us attended the same college in Maryville. We had developed a pretty tight friendship. I couldn't confide in them.

I also enjoyed art and painting in 12th grade. I lost time while painting and could express myself. I was beginning to enjoy quilting. I liked English Composition, and began writing, albeit rather dark, poems. I made straight A's in Composition. The instructor liked my style. I still have the notebook full of poems, written with a dreary and constipated style that anguishes me when I read them later. A few stanzas from one of my favorites that I wrote:

Glass City Everybody cracks (16 years old)

Here in the city is where I die

With nothing but loneliness by my side

And in my brain, my thoughts are lies

Not even worthy of tears to cry.

Happiness is not a joke.

The smile hides forgotten hope

The city plugs its damn kaleidoscope

In my eyes and ears, I lust for dope.

And far away out of reach of love

Loneliness hides in clouds above

And watches as I push and shove

And covers my body with its poison tongue

The city sits back, laughs and sees

It's starving children and hears their screams

Then sits back and smiles with glee

As its starving children drop to their knees.

The poem winds on and on just like this. The last two stanzas:

I live day to day without much meaning

All around me is a cement ceiling

Can't break through without much feeling

There's nothing-nothing too revealing

So whoever reads this, I'll call a friend

But even on you I can't depend

I lay in bed, one more night to contend

Wake up in the morning—bed's empty again.

Poems that cried for help, but no one tried to support to me. I quietly hid them. I tried turning them in, but my favorite composition teacher didn't see the inward message. I wrote one called Death. Here's the first stanza:

> Help me. I'm dying. I'm going fast.
> I want to get out of this vast mass.
> Of pollution and dust.
> It's trash that's killing me, not a person or gun.
> The world isn't big enough for me.

(Frankly, in 2022, they scare the fucking shit out of me. Nobody saw my depression or fear cause I hid it. If they had, would this book be written?)

In high school, I was horrid at math, never understood algebra and kind of good at history. Lester excelled in history and helped me with math.

As for some of the girls I knew in high school: Portia became a nurse and Denise died of a heart attack at forty. I stay in touch with my high school senior class on social media and at reunions, but reunions are hard for me socially. My other friends, Jeremy and Michael were a year or two older than I. I talk to Jeremy who lives in Kansas City.

Lester and I attended prom in the junior and senior year. Junior year wasn't as elegant, but senior year prom was sparkly and beautiful. I graduated high school in May of 1980.

During the summer in the first week of June, I went to music camp. It was at the state university in Warrensburg, MO. I stayed with other girls in a dorm who I didn't know. A couple of girls bought vodka and marijuana with them. We discussed dieting and guys and drank vodka and got high one evening. The rest of the time we spent in rehearsals.

I auditioned for music camp choir but wasn't successful. I was busy enough with orchestra. We were told not to go off campus but found ourselves at Taco Bell across the street from the college where we stayed.

Music camp was tough, and they expected perfection in the orchestra. It wasn't summer fun and games. In the end there was a concert for our parents. Then we went home.

Chapter 19

THE SHIFT

In August of 1980, at the start of college, something in my thought process shifted. That summer, in June after music camp, I worked at the opening of Les and Cooper Milk handing out samples.

    In July, my wisdom teeth were pulled. The orthodontist had to displace my jaw to remove my bottom teeth. For two weeks I lived on blended food, often watermelon or even slushies. It's all I could eat. My face swelled like a chipmunk. My jaw couldn't move. Mom had a thirty-year-old Oster blender. I wrote the word "Watermelon" on paper because I couldn't talk. Trust me when I say that watermelon blended without extra whey protein, kale or *superfood* is inedible. Why they started adding extra ingredients to something as fresh as watermelon in a smoothie is beyond me.

Sometime in the summer of 1980, I started a diet.

In August, before college started, I went with a friend down south to El Dorado, Missouri doing a job gathering petition signatures for clean energy. It was a good gig as we were paid 2 cents a signature.

El Dorado was located two hours south of Kansas City. The Clean Energy Cause meant extra cash in our pocket. Clean energy was a new concept and finally took off in the '90's. Each of us worked hard and earned over 100 dollars.

Before we started gathering signatures, we met at a small country church in El Dorado. The doors creaked opening to a hallway. The registration table was in the sanctuary. In the sanctuary there were dark wooden pews, and to the side on the white walls were 3 wooden crosses with Jesus, and on the other side of the room, three wooden crosses with Jesus. I started looking at the crosses. Each cross, the Jesus had a different expression. Cross number one, he was squinting and frowning. Cross number two, he had his mouth and eyes open in a horrific expression. Cross number three, he was smiling. On the opposite side, the crosses had the same expressions.

I thought it was rather creepy and wanted out of the church. I watched my friend who was also staring at the weird crosses.

I had just passed the violin entrance exam to be accepted at one of the "best ten music colleges in America" in Maryville. I had a career waiting for me in music therapy, I thought.

Chapter 20

SSHH DON'T TELL

While using the bathroom in the creepy little church, I talked to a couple of girls who weighed around 90 pounds, carrying their babies in their skinny arms. One wore a blue gingham dress, with an obviously flat stomach. I always admired thin girls and talked myself into a **weight goal of 95.** I've never figured out why. I looked at them. "No way," I thought. I pulled them aside and asked, "Would you tell me how you stay so thin?" And this started it all.

The thinnest girl wearing the blue gingham dress, with short brown hair, thin thigh gap legs, no curves, answered with a smile, "Thank you so much. That's such a nice compliment. I'm not supposed to tell you this, but it's from eating and throwing up. You eat regular, then you sneak to the bathroom and throw up by sticking your finger down your throat. Sometimes we eat a whole lot and then throw up. Either way, it works. You'll stay really thin. You should try it! Keep it a secret, though. Ssh Don't tell," I thanked them, and never forgot. My friend was in the other stall.

When my friend and I drove home, she said, "Did you see the weird crosses?"

"Yeah, I thought I was the only one who noticed."

I knew she heard my conversation with the skinny girls, but it was never mentioned.

Chapter 21

EDUCATED BY MIA

Lessoned learned in El Dorado, Missouri. *That's* when I met *Mia*. Remember: *Mia* is short for bulimia. *Ana* (short for anorexia) overlooked my eating disorder like a ghost, following in Mia's footsteps.

During the fall of 1980, I met *Ed. ED* is a medical abbreviation for Eating Disorder. In Pro-Ana communities online, they refer to Ed as a male. I never forgot the girls in El Dorado. To me, throwing up seemed no big deal. A sparse amount of information about eating disorders existed in 1980. If it were in a library, I had already read it.

I attended college in Maryville in 1980. Northwest Missouri State University was beautiful, unlike any buildings I had ever seen. Proud and regal red brick with white columns and white trimmed windows beautifully designed campus, historic from 1904. Some students stayed there in dorms and rode bikes all over the campus. I drove a half hour from Savannah to Maryville and walked everywhere. I covered hundreds of miles the two years I attended.

The Fine Arts building was adjacent to the theater. Next to the theater was the gymnasium and a short walk to where one of the community centers was housed. It's in this cafeteria where I ate. I could look out the window and see both the stadium and Fine Arts Theater. The campus was huge, and easy to get lost. One of my classes was so hard to find, I never attended. Makes sense, right?

Large parks surrounded the buildings, and a lot of students ate outside. The campus had at least four dorms, though I never counted. My favorite building was the library, down the street from the stadium and Fine Arts building.

When I toured Northwest Missouri State University with my family, we were awestruck. Savannah didn't have anything this beautiful. The few times I'd visited Kansas City, I never saw anything like the buildings at Northwest Missouri State University.

Northwest Missouri State University in Maryville was thirty minutes from Iowa. As close as we lived to Iowa, I'd never been. Some of the students went to Iowa on regular occasions into Des Moines for shopping.

Personally, I'd rather go into Kansas City at the Country Club Plaza.

The air at the university was so fresh that it invited students to be outside. The air blew through the trees and made the grass move in green waves. The sun shined with beautiful hues of yellow and orange. Even though Savannah was full of agriculture, Northwest Missouri State University was clean, crisp and very green.

There was a farm, disconnected from the main university, with a pond so blue that reflections were mirrored. Everything about the university was paradise. But paradise can be a broken mirror.

Chapter 22

AVOIDING THE SOPHOMORE TWENTY

Lester decided to take a semester off from college in Utah, to help his dad with Les and Cooper milk. Lester still insisted on going to Utah University, even though Maryville developed an agricultural program. He was unimpressed and focused on his dad's milk company. He still seemed to care about me, but after high school, he changed. When I attended the Maryville University, it was the first time in 2 years I'd been separated from him.

At home, I started weighing myself about once a week. I refused to gain the sophomore twenty. All the girls at the university in the gym locker room and even in the cafeteria center talked about the sophomore twenty. I heard plenty of ways to avoid it, including purging, bingeing and purging, and drastic dieting. One of the girls had laxatives in her purse which totally repulsed me, (for a while). I made my mom buy me a new bathroom scale the first week I started classes.

  I decided to change what I ate for lunch, which was a turkey sandwich, apple and Tab. It took me awhile to decide to make the change. I heard the conversations in the cafeteria regarding weight from college girls I didn't know but shared a table. I was shy and quiet, unable to approach others to ask if I could sit with them. I paid attention and heard every conversation around my table. I had an uncanny ability to know what every person around me said.

"Damn, my pants are too tight," or "I better not eat today, I'm gaining," were common phrases.

"No way, no cookies for me."

Jeremy from high school saw me sitting alone in the large cafeteria. We began to eat lunch together. Actually, I preferred to sit with Jeremy for more intelligent conversations, but our lunch only occurred at the same time three days a week. The other two days I sat alone listening to discussions.

"Did you do your assignment for music theory?" he'd ask, condescending. "Yeah, I did," I reassured him. He was in a few classes with me, in the fine arts building.

"What are you eating? Gotta make damn sure you eat more than three apples," he would say remembering high school days. (Why the hell would he pay attention to what I ate in high school? Besides, it was 6 apples, so he thought.) It remained an unfunny joke except I really *did* eat three apples when I sat alone. "But I ate 6 apples a day in high school, Jeremy." I said, reminding him.

"Turkey sandwich, apple and a Tab." I answered, showing him my plate. The sandwich was turkey on a large onion bun.

At least there was one apple.

Soon my diet changed. I began to restrict calories but didn't realize I was cutting calories. I thought *restricting* which was a term I read in a women's magazine at the grocery store meant I didn't eat certain foods together. To me restriction meant you'd eat a protein and a carb but not a sugary carb like a cookie. So, you'd restrict the extra carb. It was complicated.

It was my understanding, that low carb restriction diet meant something to this effect: If you ate a cookie carb, you'd not eat a bread carb, but you could eat a protein without a fat. If you ate a protein with a bread carb, you'd skip the cookie carb because you were eating a fruit carb. Then you'd have to add a fat because you skipped the cookie carb. Welcome to early '80's diet books. I tried organizing that concept, but it became an awful algebra equation.

I don't know why I didn't associate restriction to *cutting* calories. I occasionally heard the word "restriction" when listening to conversations at lunch. One girl thought she ate too much and "restricted". All I did was watch my calories. I dug out the tiny, now yellowing with age, Dell booklet, *"Counting Calories"* and carried it in my purse.

One day, I realized what restricting was and began to slowly cut out my calories. Though still complicated, it got easier with time. I'd noticed a dizzy feeling when I didn't consume food. In truth, it was low blood sugar not replaced. Then the dizziness went away, and my head was clear. I usually had candy with me to cure the feeling of faint, brought on by dizziness caused by no food. I liked the feeling of absence of food. I thought I was doing something to improve what I perceived as "my fat body". The only person I could see as obese, was me. Absence of food felt light and feminine, like a ballerina.

One day at lunch, I ordered a turkey sandwich and a can of tab, skipping the apple. If I played this right, I wouldn't need to eat dinner because I was *restricting*. It was fashionable. But what was the trick, and did it work? Did the girls in El Dorado make excuses at dinner, "I had a big lunch, sorry, not hungry."

"Where's your apple?" Jeremy asked, looking at the one lonely sandwich on my tray next to a can of Tab.

"I'm full. I had a big breakfast," total lie because I skipped breakfast. I was experimenting a tactic that I made up, and it worked.

This became my excuse that I used for years to not eat meals. I don't know how I came up with this excuse, but it worked every time. Out of my mouth the words floated words so smooth, "I had a big breakfast," when all I really had was a Tab.

Sometimes for breakfast, I ate cheese and peanut butter crackers with my can of Tab. At the grocery store once, I read a lady's magazine and got the idea that cheese and peanut butter crackers along with a can of Tab were too much food (190 calories), because of the fat content of the peanut butter. Then I tried adding up the calories of one cheese and peanut butter cracker, instead of the whole pack. The cracker pack had 190. 190 divided by 6 is what? The answer wasn't in my head and the cracker package didn't say. When I got home, I found the answer was 31. THIS is the day I began to add calories of packaged foods and dividing the amount down to a piece. One Skittle had 4 calories. One Oreo was 53 calories. I took the time to figure out everything I had that was prepacked and listed the calories down to one item.

If I had an apple with my sandwich, I thought I got too full. Of course, I talked myself into the fact that I thought I was full. The extra 95 calories can't be good. Calories make me fat and apple were a carb. If I got hungry during the day, I'd get cheese and peanut butter crackers from the vending machine or suffer through it. Apples got juice on my clothes and weren't worth the effort.

Chapter 23

THE PLAN

A purge is forced vomiting after eating. Removal and expulsion are two synonyms of purging. My first purge was in September of 1980. The afternoon of my first purge, my stomach was in a solid knot, and it felt like it was frozen with undigested food. It takes food to create peristalsis. There was no food, no peristalsis. My stomach felt full and uncomfortable. I had eaten a turkey sandwich from the cafeteria at college. For dessert, I had an apple that I didn't always eat and drank a Tab from the vending machine. My limited diet was beginning to have side effects: constant constipation, unable to create intestinal peristalsis, and slow digestion.

I was practically eating one meal a day. If I got hungry at home, I ate an apple. My excuse at home continued to be "I ate a big lunch." I didn't learn these excuses from anyone, I made them up and they continued to work like a charm. Sometimes I changed the wording to, "We had a huge buffet catered to us by a Mexican restaurant." Then I went on to recreate that supposed buffet complete with enchiladas, tacos, nachos, Mexican rice.

In October, I switched to cake or cheese and peanut butter crackers and an apple for lunch. The apple on my tray was a decoy. It went either in the trash or in my backpack for when I got home. The turkey sandwich was too much food according to me. Jeremy would roll his eyes or have an expression of concern. "We're going to have a talk one day about your food, young lady."

I remember time, I was having a nice conversation at lunch, with Jeremy, in the Community building. We were facing a large open balcony and had a beautiful view of the city of Maryville. We could see one of the city parks. In the park was a large mystical pond. Fog drifted over the water. It was nice to stare at the pond and meditate, until a goose flew out of the drifting fog and darted towards the window where we held a deep gaze. A gaggle of geese were often fed by college students who ate lunches outside across the street, so much for meditation. It was a beautiful but humorous landscape. The fact that it was meditative gave our minds a break from classes.

  Jeremy said, "You completely lose your thoughts by staring at the fog."

Not my thoughts. My brain wouldn't stop thinking. Think, think, think, think, think. Years later I learned to stop my thoughts through deep meditation. But in my freshman year at college, my mind wouldn't stop. "How do I get rid of this food? I ate too much. How many calories again?" haunted thoughts I couldn't stop.

I started making excuses to cut lunch short.

"Jeremy, I have to go practice violin with Elin." Elin was first chair violinist in orchestra, I was her partner. "I also need to stop at the library, see you later. Call me."

He had no reason to doubt me as I spent a lot of time in the college library.

I didn't preplan purging, it seemed to be done on impulse. I decided I had eaten too much food and had to get rid of it before I absorbed the calories.

The thought I created repeated itself, "You ate too damn much. Get rid of it. You keep putting food in your stomach, you'll be a fat pig."

"Oh shit," I thought and almost said it out loud. "I have to get rid of this food. How can I do it quick?" I was at a table in the Community building adjacent to the fine arts building. And that's how it started.

Chapter 24

THE PURGE

"Jeremy, I have to run and make copies at the Fine Arts Building. See you later." I thought quickly enough to say, "Fine Arts Building". I reiterated in case he was able to see me walk in that direction. The next time we met for lunch, I viewed the route and realized we were facing the other side of the parking lot.

"Okay sweetie." (He always called me sweetie. No one called me baby. I wanted to be called baby by at least one guy. I didn't care who. I would think no one cared enough about me to call me "Baby.")

After lunch that day, I dashed to the Fine Arts building. It was about a quarter mile walk through a parking lot and then into the theater door which connected with the Fine Arts unit. I located a private bathroom. It was clear on the opposite side of the building in a dark alcove near some stairs. I eye-balled the private bathroom weeks before.

I traipsed into the low-lit alcove after pausing to see if anyone watched. Girls who are bulimic know all the public bathrooms, all the private bathrooms, exactly how many stalls, often what time bathrooms are cleaned. Girls who are bulimic are mysterious and secretive. I had no idea I was bulimic but felt embarrassed about getting caught.

The private bathroom was empty and smelled of Lysol. I opened the door, crept in, and locked the doorknob and flipped on the light. The hall dimmed but the bathroom light shined bright yellow. The common technique I used must've been preplanned in my brain. I knew how to force vomit, from the girls in El Dorado. It felt like someone behind me methodically told me each step. I was flawless from running the warm water in the beginning to rinsing out my mouth at the end.

    I had long brown spiraled hair, so I made sure it was not near my face. I ran warm water in the sink that sat in front of the toilet. I left the faucet on for noise. I wet my right index and middle fingers in warm running water and lifted the toilet lid with my left hand. I squatted in front of the toilet and jammed the index and middle finger of my right hand down my throat, feeling the opening of my esophagus. The esophageal tissue felt like a firm opening but the tissue around the esophagus was soft and flimsy. The oral cavity wanted to close on my fingers before they reached the esophagus opening. My tongue felt larger than its actual size. The back of my tongue felt swollen and tried to cover my fingers unsuccessfully.

    I visualized the light fuchsia colored esophagus, what it looked like, how it felt, and I created a gag reflux by tickling my fingers against the delicate opening. The opening of the upper esophagus allowed room for the tickle and gag of my middle finger. The sphincter at the esophagus entrance felt soft, watery, with a medium orifice into the esophageal cavity. I could feel the thin, firm tissue of the muscular opening. I was surprised how far into the throat my middle finger reached. I shoved my fingers down my throat causing a reflux reaction that brought stomach contents up through my mouth into the toilet. I saw undigested turkey sandwich floating in the toilet. Second gag. I saw the apple undigested along with the Tab. While anyone else would be repulsed by the appearance of self-induced vomitus in floating in a toilet, I thought nothing of it.

I stared at the undigested chunks of chewed food, floating and, glorious! Out of my stomach came the undigested then digested turkey sandwich, in bits. It took several amounts of forced gagging by my fingers to get rid of the undigested food stuck between my esophagus and stomach. Each gag seemed as fluid as the first. Timewise, it didn't take long at all. It was a blessing or a curse that I wasn't loud so no one could even guess.

I stood up and looked into the toilet bowl, watching floating undigested stomach content. I flushed the toilet completely three times. It smelled, for a moment, like vomit, but with each flush, the stench disappeared. I smelled my fingers. They had a strong vile scent of vomit, like the toilet. Even after washing my hands, they still kind of smelled of vomit. That's just one of the things, I thought. Later I went to the school store and bought scented hand lotion for my backpack.

Often in a household of a bulimic, one of the problems is plumbing. The chewed food is vomited in large pieces. It does not go down the toilet correctly and plugs the pipes. Also repeated vomiting can cause grease to build up in the pipes. If a plumber is called, the food contents are discovered, as is the secret. Also. the food contents smells of exactly what it is: old undigested food. The smell lingers in the bathroom. That was always my fear, but no worries in a public toilet.

I ran warm water on my face, washed my hands, did a make-up check in the mirror. My lips smelled like vomit, so I reapplied the lipstick and swished water around my mouth, spit it down the sink and left the private bathroom feeling successful and euphoric. I grabbed a mint from my purse. The feeling after self-induced vomiting the first time was ecstatic. It was like I was lifted into a strange realm, meditative and flowing above everyone I saw in the hallway. The feeling lasted several hours.

I went to the college library the same week to search books about self-induced vomiting. I didn't have a name for what I did. I wanted to read about other people who did the same thing. There wasn't adequate information in the library. What I had accomplished was genius and secretive and triumphant. No one knew but me. My weight would be controlled forever this way! I got on the scales the next morning and pleasingly discovered I lost a couple of pounds. The first purge was successful.

In 1980, there wasn't available written information regarding eating disorders, so I developed my own habits. I tweaked and developed ideas to avoid or get rid of food (purging) and wrote them in a notebook. If this doesn't move the scales down, this will work.

Lester remained busy and focused with his dad's business. I often helped out on the weekends but had too much homework and my papers had to be pristine to me. I kept my grades up, except for the one class I couldn't find on campus. I flunked that class.

I was friends with people I ran around with in high school, but even distanced myself from them. They thought I was on hard drugs because I was getting so skinny. The only friend who hung with me by my side was Jeremy. Lester never mentioned me being too skinny, but my priority was my homework in music theory and practicing. I didn't let him see my stomach and he had no idea how I looked.

My friends, Jeremy and Michael from high school, tried offering me pizza which I refused. "You turned down pizza?" they said with their mouths agape staring with again, the look of concern. Jeremy seemed most worried, "You shouldn't turn down pizza. You're already too skinny." And often patted my stomach. I dressed in layers; he couldn't touch my ribs. I wasn't skinny, not to me. "But my thighs", I felt like screaming to them. Once I said out loud, "But my thighs." Jeremy said, "You're not going to have anything but bones on your thighs." Again, I starved without a crazy amount of exercising, running, or other sorts of activity. The only real activity I did was walking to my classes.

In the mirror at home, my clavicles and ribs were protruding, so I meticulously hid them. I wanted my clavicles and ribs to protrude in the mirror but didn't want anyone to see. It was a goal, but I never considered myself skinny. Another male friend from high school I saw in orchestra at the university, a cellist named Hans, gently expressed concern and softly said one day, "You don't eat. You're going to succumb to not eating. I think you need help." It's not the first time someone would mention help. It thought I was fine.

Chapter 25

ORCHESTRATED

I had a few college friends, a couple I'm still friends with, several who died. A couple of male friends from college, died of AIDS in the late '80's. My friend, Elin, and I were violin partners in orchestra. She was incredibly talented. She could sight read, and memorized music so fast as if she had been given the music and studied for months. She had long reddish hair and a wonderful spirit.

Elin kind of looked in on me during orchestra. "Did you practice? Do you know your part?" I often looked her in the eye and tried to figure out if she knew my behavior. I purged my cake a half an hour ago, don't give me shit. I did spend a lot of time practicing in the practice rooms in the basement. That way, I didn't have to see people. They also made great study rooms where I could catch up on reading.

  Once in class Elin tried to tell me how to play a bar of notes. When everything was quiet, I told her to fuck off. We never lost touch and laugh at it today.

When orchestra had a fall picnic at one of the parks in Maryville near the university, there was a cooler of beer. I wasn't 21 but enjoyed indulging. As little as I was, it didn't take much alcohol to get me drunk. I strolled down to a creek, and saw a dead body, and told the teacher. He called the police. The picnic had turned into a party with marijuana and drinking. As soon as our instructor called the police, the party dispersed.

College had constant movement and started having weird vibes. There was drinking, pot, parties where I would find instructors smoking pot and drinking. It became a circle or a dead end.

A particular party was at a stranger's house. I was invited by Jeremy. He seemed ultra-caring and watchful. I'm sure he didn't know the half of it, nor have I ever told him.

I met Jeremy at the house party. It was a huge historical house in a neighborhood where mostly students lived. Jeremy was the utmost gentleman. He grabbed me by the arm and introduced me to everyone. I was surprised Elin wasn't there, or maybe she attended, and I didn't know.

I was offered hot buttered rum. The butter was heated over an open fire in the backyard. The party was close to Halloween, and someone was walking around dressed like a pumpkin.

A whiff of the sour sweet smell of marijuana permeated the air. I was drinking hot buttered rum from a large mug. In the corner of my eye, I saw my English instructor with a joint. It made me laugh even harder when he offered it to me, which I accepted. I passed it to Jeremy, who passed it to someone else. The Grateful Dead's Sugar Magnolia was playing in the background. Marijuana ran rampant in the university. There was a lot of farmlands with rumors that the best weed came from "up north."

(I loved hot buttered rum, and have tried making it since, but mine doesn't exactly taste like the hot buttered rum I had at the party.)

In October through December, I was purging in the same bathroom regularly. Always running lukewarm water in the sink, and carefully flushing the stomach contents down the toilet three times. I checked my make up (self-induced vomiting can cause blood vessels to break in the face), reapplied my lipstick, and washed my hands. After this I used scented hand lotion, and by now carried a bottle of cheap perfume in my backpack. I sprayed after I vomited to cover the putrid smell. Then I sucked on a peppermint to hide my revolting vomit breath.

Once I got digested stomach contents on a pink blouse, coating my chest and my bra with liquid, smelly, stomach contents. I could smell the repugnant odor on my skin. Always prepared, there was an extra shirt in my car. I threw away the vomit coated blouse in the university trash and covered up the rancid smell with perfume.

It was a constant challenge of getting "rid" of the food, even though there were risks involved. I was lucky I didn't get caught.

On days I knew I'd purge; I ate a turkey sandwich. I discovered other foods that were easier to purge, two being ice cream or milk shakes. The bun on the turkey sandwich sometimes came up in dense pieces and hurt my esophagus. Cake was soft and came up easily without much force. Apples were difficult because they were a harder food but had moist interior. Turkey sandwiches weren't the easiest because the bread was dense. I would think at night in bed that if I drank more water between bites, it would be easier to bring up the turkey sandwich. This is the list I made of food to try for successful purging.

Ice cream

Mashed potato or baked potato with topping

Peanut butter

Crackers with tons of water

Banana

Yellow cake with chocolate frosting, which they had in the cafeteria

Cream pie which they sometimes sold in the cafeteria

Pasta with spaghetti sauce though it would be harder to get the stains off my fingers and I would have to make sure to wear something black.

Grapes or blackberries

Bananas as long as they were soft

One can of Tab, water or iced tea.

I made this list in a notebook and carried it with me, adding food or crossing off food that didn't work for purging. I made notes by the entries. ("95 calories" "Damn, spaghetti sauce shows on my black shirt.")

In a perfect world, this list was limited food, but not a lousy list of food choices if one chooses a different path. Granted it was missing vegetables and fruit, but they were difficult to purge without choking, or caused me to be able to vomit the entire meal because I ate broccoli. At night, I calculated each calorie. I edited my lunch list down to yellow cake (skip the frosting), or cheese and peanut butter crackers chased with Tab. Sometimes a banana would work quite well if I drank water afterwards. Ice cream would seem odd in front of Jeremy. He knew my allergies.

    I developed my food list around my allergies, and the food that was easiest to purge. Ice cream and cake was by far the easiest food to purge, ending up nice and smooth in the toilet. It usually flushed twice with no evidence. Cake was smoothly purged. It left no chunks in the toilet and didn't smell as bad afterwards. By itself, cake left a toilet full of floating yellow, wet powder. It smelled like sweet vomit, but nothing too sour or putrid.

I didn't think I needed to cover up the smell with cheap perfume. (I probably wreaked of sweet vomit.)

This is when I changed my lunch *again* to just cheese and peanut butter crackers and a Tab. To make my meal complete in front of Jeremy, I bought an apple or banana. Sometimes I ate cake, but I didn't care for taste of the chocolate frosting.

Cake, Part two, the frosting…When the frosting was thrown up, it made my mouth feel greasy and the chocolate tasted bitter. My fingernails stayed greasy all day long, as it didn't wash well with the soap in the bathroom. Frosting was too much of a mess to deal with.

When I bought cake at the cafeteria, I bought 2 pieces, and removed the frosting before eating. The premise on buying two pieces was, I needed something to eat, even though I focused on calories. I was able to hide the frosting in my napkin, and still eat with Jeremy watching. It was easy, I waited for him to turn around, or look down or get up. I swear he never saw me wipe the frosting off the cake. I chased the cake with Tab and made an excuse to get to class early so I could hurry to the private bathroom in the other building. I hurried, running to the Fine Arts building because, again, cake digested quicker than any of the food on my list.

That described my purging days. I knew better than to puke every day, because it was unhealthy. Makes sense, right? On other days, I counted calories, I calculated servings and other what not. I thought counting calories *was* healthy. Everybody counted calories. It was in every woman's magazine and entire books were written around calories of foods.

As an afterthought, I never asked Jeremy if he thought I was bulimic. I think I hid it very well.

On revolving days, Jeremy and I had two different lunch times. It was easier to go downstairs in the Fine Arts Building break area instead of running to the Community building. I began to hang around dancers in the Fine Arts Building break area. They ate in the basement break area near the vending machines where I bought my morning Tab.

There was a small table, a few chairs, a soda machine and snack machine. Down the hall were the ballet class rooms. The instructor sometimes peaked out at the students. She was tiny, and strong. She had long flowing brown hair that she kept tied in a purple scrunchy. She wore black tights, black ballet shoes, a cotton skirt, and purple ballet sweater tied at the waist. She walked with the grace of the prima ballerina she once was, pointing her toes as she graced the hallway.

This motivated me to start dancing, again, on my own. I started taking ballet at a private studio at the university taught by one of the students. A male dancer assured me, "Take ballet so you don't have to eat."

I began to change how I ate *again*. Instead of purging, I began to feel the need not to eat. Not eating left, me empty and something occurred in my brain with my neurotransmitters. (I still get the same feeling today when I feel that "ED" is going to return.) It feels like a sudden brain depletion of serotonin, and then the neurotransmitters are activated by the feeling when I see something that triggers the sensation. I tested my brain at times, noting if I missed purging, when I felt the need to purge, and what I ate that set off the feeling. I had purged so often I started to miss it.

In one of my classes, it was erroneously titled, "Stretch and Move." It was a pre-dance credit. With a class named Stretch and Move you can only imagine.

I didn't have a beautiful ballerina for a teacher in Stretch and Move, as I expected, but a woman who appeared to be a weightlifter instead. She had a hard manly disposition and a hefty stride. She walked up to me while I was sitting straddle legged on a mat, and said, "You have too much thigh flab, so you need to stretch more." I could see a pattern from junior high. (Huh? I take ballet.) I couldn't speak, but stared at her in the blankest, deepest, hurtful expression. I believed her, and that one phrase, sealed it.

I was fat, needed to get skinny, and knew how. The girls from the El Dorado, MO bathroom were right. I weighed 118, my lowest. I had obviously already started the motions into full on anorexia-bulimia.

I began to make notes in my notebook, and calculated food calories into single portions, as I had started doing in high school. This helped manage the calorie count. What happened was: when I counted calories, my body knew it needed food. When I didn't count calories, I puked everything into the toilet. As I walked to my classes, I obsessed over what to eat, even though I knew I'd get cheese and peanut butter crackers and Tab. Counting calories made me *hungrier*. It was not the route to take nor was it healthy, nor was any route I took healthy.

On days I didn't count calories, I felt like a whale full of stuffing that needed to be removed. If I counted calories, I maintained my weight. If I didn't count calories, I gained. A very dangerous circle began to occur. Counting calorie- no gain, not counting calories-gain, purge-no gain, counting calories-no gain, not counting calories-gain and so on, like a dog chasing his tail.

Regretful and defeated, I started purging, but only a couple of days a week. One month, I skipped purging. I missed the feeling. I journaled everything, and every food that made me full, made me hungry and was an easy purge.

Chapter 26

ELECTION FAIL

Maryville had windy fall seasons. The trees were beautiful in fall foliage colors of brown, red, dark green. I had little body fat, and the air made my bones chill. I started wearing a sweatshirt, under the sweatshirt I wore a t-shirt, and under a t-shirt I wore a tank top. I walked so much outside; I easily hit 5 to 7 miles a day while in class.

    Savannah's trees changed with the seasons, and when the fall colors returned every year, there were orange, brown and purple leaves. Savannah had a huge fall fest with fall food, pumpkin pie and pumpkin bread. My family attended every year. Often, I met Jeremy there and we would eat pumpkin bread or pumpkin pie under a beautiful oak tree in the process of changing the leave colors for fall. It was a beautiful festival. The cinnamon smelled delightful. There was hot apple cider and hot buttered rum, though I wasn't old enough to buy liquor. Jeremy and I settled for hot cider and pumpkin pie.

I already spotted the porta potties placed by the City of Savannah. I was actively purging, even on the weekends, if I could. I figured pumpkin pie would be easier to purge than pumpkin bread. I got a huge, uncharacteristic piece of pumpkin pie. Jeremy said, "Well that piece is impressive."

Fresh homemade pie was always a treat. I chose a picnic table close to the porta-potties. Of course, my thoughts, eat fast, and dash to the bathroom, and don't look into the toilet. I opened the porta-potty door and I squeezed myself down to a squat on the floor and faced the plastic dirty toilet, glanced at the contents, ignored the smell of feces and urine and whatever pungency lurked down there in the toilet bowl. I covered the toilet contents with toilet paper so I couldn't see, closed my eyes and made myself gag. Pumpkin pie took only 2 times jamming my finger down my throat. It vomited easily and effortlessly, even without the traditional warm water on my fingers to assist the contents upward through the esophagus. I watched as undigested chewed pumpkin pie landed on the top of the contents of the porta-potty. I threw some toilet paper on top to cover the evidence. Once out of the porta-potty, I cleaned my hands with the water fountain and hope I didn't smell like vomit.

Purging in a porta-potty could've been my worse bulimic episode. Bulimia never stops and follows you wherever you are. It doesn't allow the victim to discriminate what is wrong and what is normal. Its goal is simply, get the food out no matter what.

Jeremy and I walked around to the rides, even rode the Ferris wheel like everything was normal. In a bizarre world, it wasn't.

It was October, and the election was heated. The race was between Jimmy Carter and Ronald Reagan. My dad said, "That Reagan son of a bitch. This house votes democrat." He put a Jimmy Carter sign in our front yard. Andrew County was neutral, as part of it voted democrat, and the other republican.

I was so excited to vote. It would be my first time to really make a difference. In November 1980, I voted in my first presidential election. I felt like my vote would change the world. I went into the voting booth and selected for Jimmy Carter. I voted straight democrat. My parents took the Maryville paper, and I got up early the next morning to read the election results. Carter lost. (I still don't understand THAT one.) I was devastated. It felt like a knife went through my chest the next morning when reading the headlines: "Reagan Wins in a Landslide." A landslide, no fucking way.

The cover of Time Magazine had a picture of Reagan (I called him Ray-gun), which read "A fresh start." My thought process said, "A step back, we're in trouble." Though I hadn't a clue until we had full internet and the stats, facts and figures were available. In 1980, I thought I could've done more, and had no idea how to get involved. If more people voted, this could've gone in a different direction.

At the time of this writing, I stay up until the loosing opponent concedes, watching every election moment on television, and online.

Chapter 27

PIANO PLAYS THE BLUES

In college, my Piano 101 class was phenomenal. The teacher, who I got to know on a first name basis, Calvin Smith, was one of my favorites. He tried to make a difference in my life beyond piano technique. He was a soft spoken, caring, large, framed man, balding hair and glasses. He was probably about 10 years older than me. I am still grateful for his caring and presence. He lived near the college, by himself.

The class was after lunch. I had to walk a mile to the building. There were five people in the class, and it was personalized. Two Asian girls named Casey and Cici, George, Hank and me. On our first day of class,

Calvin, "Mr. Smith" introduced himself as "Calvin, and please call me Calvin."

He had us group in a small circle, say our names and something we liked to do, and what was our major. Casey and Cici were both majoring in piano. George, musical theater. Hank's hobby was writing music and needed to take Piano 101. I said, "Painting and reading.'

Calvin said, "I'm very personal in this class. I will sit next to you and stand behind you for obvious reasons. It's a piano class, but I like to get to know you on a personal basis. I'm not picky on what you play for Monday's assignments, but I do ask that you are here every class period, and that you make an effort to do the work."

On Monday the choice of music didn't matter. On Fridays we performed Monday's assignment. Wednesday was technique class with scales, arpeggios.

Calvin spoke to each of us when we went to class and complimented something he noticed. Sometimes it was more of a concern than a compliment. On Monday, He always asked us about our weekend. We performed Monday's assignment. He went around to each student, sat beside them, and corrected their form. Casey and Cici played harsh and loud, as if they were banging on a drum. The sound reverberated up to the high ceiling and down through our chairs. They played so loud, I tried to crunch my ears into my shoulders which never diminished loud noises, but I tried it anyway. I still was intolerable to loud noises, and I tried to I avoid them.

Anything excruciating gnawed my ears. I couldn't avoid the loud piano playing in the classroom.

When Calvin was assisting another student, we read, waited our turn, or studied. Most of the students read. I waited, observed. I lightly tapped my foot if I had to wait too long for something.

On our first week we had to tell him the song we would play for our piano proficiency at the end of semester, for his approval.

I preferred rock music. Calvin allowed me to play a blues arrangement of "Goin' to Kansas City" written in 1955 by Fats Domino. I bought the sheet music at a local store in Maryville a few months before piano class. I practiced and wrote a blues arrangement. This is what I played for my piano proficiency in

December, and I made an A. Maybe the whole class made A's.

The piano classes were located in an old church converted into classrooms. The University bought the old church and didn't make too many improvements to restore it. They filled it with pianos and made it into a classroom.

The building was on the haunted buildings list a few years later. A trained paranormal investigator verified that ghosts originally lived in the building. Occasionally the ghosts wafted throughout the old church making creaky sounds. It was said the ghosts were those of the people whose funerals took place there in the 1800's. There were crevices of warm patches, and swift cold air brushed our shoulders during certain songs.

The classroom had nine pianos, two baby grands, 3 uprights, and 4 mini uprights, and 2 grand pianos. Calvin preferred we alternate between styles of piano at every class session.

It was almost a two mile walk to the old church from the fine arts building. I utilized the walk to burn off calories. The college had travel shuttles for the students if they cared to ride to go from class to class. I loved the outside air and oxygen I used to walk to class. I could connect and sync with my breath, though, my breathing was altered from purging. The building was up a hill and occasionally I ran up the incline and walked down the decline. The breath the run took to do this was difficult. My cheeks, bloodshot from the previous purge, I blamed the incline. It usually worked. "Sorry, I ran the incline," I'd say huffing out words.

Chapter 28

CATCH ME IF YOU CAN

I planned to purge after lunch on Mondays, Wednesdays and Fridays. It's not uncommon for bulimic victims to plan their binges and purges, but I have never binged. I just decided the days I would throw up, and the other days keep calories around 500.

One day for lunch, I had 2 pieces of cake, an apple, cheese and peanut butter crackers and a tab and a dirty look for Jeremy. I started adding a little more food cause cake and an apple were a too small amount to purge. My gut would tighten, and my body tried to grab what food I had given it, without allowing me to evacuate the contents. The next step would be throwing up blood and I didn't want to get that far.

"Weird lunch," he said, casting a troubled look, shaking his head and shrugging his shoulders.

On my plate were 2 beautiful pieces of yellow cake, professionally frosted. I was to the point I didn't care if he saw me remove the frosting. This was around the end of November 1980. My excuse for removing the frosting was, "Yuck, this frosting tastes like glue." I think he agreed, and I was probably correct in that assumption.

When lunch was over, I dashed outside, to the Fine Arts building, through the side door to the bathroom in the alcove. I shut the bathroom door. It smelled like Lysol and cleaning fluid. Inside the toilet were blue bubbles floating from the cleaner. I ran the warm water in the sink and turned to the toilet to squat. I stuck my middle and index finger down my throat. By now purging was mindless. I thought I was a pro.

  The cake and tab came up from my stomach easily and created a powdered brown product in the toilet. I always checked what I left in the toilet, what if I vomited blood? I stood up to wash my hands and felt dizzy. While washing my hands, I felt dizzy again. I was wearing a purple t-shirt and noticed vomited cake product dripping down my chest. I tried to clean it with water. I managed to get too much water on my shirt. I lifted my soaked shirt to check for smells. It smelled disgusting, like vomit, not cake. I didn't have any perfume with me. I looked in the mirror. My eyes were red, face was flushed. I felt so dizzy that I left the bathroom to go sit on a chair in the foyer. Around this time, I'd started getting progressively dizzier after purging.

Dizziness is a bad sign. This is a good stopping spot to discuss what I've seen in movies about girls with eating disorders, since I experienced firsthand and wrote this book.

(A quick echo of my present thoughts about movies and eating disorders: Purging messes with electrolytes and eventually blood pressure and blood sugar. It can cause dizziness, which is common, and can be deadly. I think about the way bulimia is displayed in movies, and I get irritated. In the movies, the girl (always a girl), passes out and is found by her best friend, or sister, or her family. She gets rushed to the emergency room then receives expensive treatment that

costs thousands of dollars and comes out of treatment cautiously okay. She's fine!

Or this is the moment in the movie where the girl passes out and dies. I've not seen any movie where the girl almost passes out and goes on, continuing as before. Either passes out, gets treatment, or passes out and dies. In Hollywood, there's no line between the 2. No one almost passes out and goes on living normally, if there is a normal. Hollywood and that includes Netflix and any other producer who are making movies about eating disorders, has it wrong. Note: in 2022, if a patient eats normally, and occasionally purges, it's called "purging disorder", and it's equally as deadly as bulimia.)

Sitting on a chair in the Fine Arts Building foyer, dizzy, I thought I needed a banana and water. There wasn't time to go to the cafeteria and buy a banana. I was about to fall over and crash.

Bananas sort of replenish electrolytes and sugar but not fast enough. Powerade or Gatorade does an immediate job. Sometimes I was able to grab a Gatorade from the cafeteria, but never red colored, what if I vomited blood? I bought blue Gatorade, or green, and sometimes purple.

I sat in the chair in the foyer, the room spinning. I never passed out, but there was always that danger. If I'd passed out, my head would've hit the tile flooring beneath my feet. After the dizziness subsided, thinking nothing about my appearance, I walked as fast as I could to piano class.

I felt so gross in piano class, with a wet shirt with a stain of vomit and red eyes. (Can you imagine the smell?) Calvin gently expressed concern but didn't ask. He just made a weird face. Well, I didn't look like my bright self, if there was a bright self. The next time I purged, which I could do rather fast and usually slick, I hurried, with perfume in my backpack. Smart move, but sometimes vomit odor lingered on my fingers.

Every piano class, my eyes were bloodshot, and the skin flushed around my forehead. I knew I smelled but covered that up (probably didn't cover up the smell). I never liked to smell, and that is the worse part of bulimia. My cheeks were puffy, and nose was red. Some days my voice sounded gritty, and I couldn't clear my throat. In other words, I looked like shit.

Calvin had enough of staring at my general appearance. On the day he didn't grimace, looking over his glasses he said, "Uh, Rhonda, is there something wrong?" Usually, he complimented me. (*Shit. Not today. He knows. I'm fucking doomed. Mom and dad will find out.*) I stared at him. I was stunned and annoyed, not to mention violated. I felt like I was caught. What would I do? I couldn't get myself out of this one, so I said, "Oh, I ran up the incline, and this time I ran down the incline, hard run."

He shook his head no. "You're not wearing running shoes; you're wearing black clogs."

"Yes. These are like my running shoes," He was correct. I wasn't wearing Nike running shoes; I was wearing black leather clogs. And I could run fast in them, but the concept wasn't there. "I can run really fast in these," trying to do anything to cover up. If I ran fast in them, the clogs fell off.

"No," he said. And silence.

Well. Shit. I started to tremble.

"What class do you have after mine?"

"Algebra but I never go. I'm flunking it," true.

He rolled his eyes. "I'm going to get you out of algebra. My free time is after this class. I want you to stay after. We're going to talk."

Well fuck. Now what?

I sat at the piano and almost cried. Hank who overheard the conversation with Calvin said, "Ha ha, yer in trouble young lady," he had a southern drawl. A lot of people from Savannah had a southern drawl, even Lester sometimes.

I sulked the whole class, robotically did my scales and arpeggios.

After class, Calvin and I had a very long talk. Every time I had piano class, I stayed over to talk. Classes were Monday, Wednesday and Friday at 1:05. The hour after piano class was his free period. I was pretty sure I wasn't missed in algebra. The algebra instructor didn't give a shit if you showed up or not.

When Calvin approached me on this particular day, it was 15 minutes after the purge. I'd been purging about three times a week for almost three months. I was restricting calories, 500, or one meal a day when I didn't purge. My lunch time was straight up 12. I quickly ate lunch at the Community center, walked out the doors to a sidewalk, up a hill to the Fine Arts Building, winding around to the private bathroom, and purged. Then I'd run up the sidewalk incline, walked down the sidewalk, which was a large hill, to Calvin's class. It was that fast.

Unobvious to me, I had no idea how Calvin could sense an ensuing problem. Maybe my cheeks were puffy, forehead flushed. I hadn't learned to carry Visine in my purse for my eyes. I was very careful to not burst blood vessels when I purged, but there was often a flushed appearance that wasn't normal on a regular 18-year-old girl. The flushed appearance exhibited tiny blood vessels that I'm sure would be noticeable only to someone educated. Make-up couldn't always disguise signs. Puffy thin cheeks are a sign of purging. I was skinny, little wrists and ankles. I looked about 12. To anyone else, my face was round, thin but puffy. I thought my butt was huge. My face looked like a chipmunk. Plus, my Stretch and Move instructor said I had fat thighs in front of *everyone*, and instructors don't lie. Oh my god, I hope I hope I didn't smell.

I found out Calvin was only five years older than I. He wore glasses, slacks or jeans and plaid button up shirts.

"Honey," he asked after class.

"Yeah," I answered timid and wanting to hide somewhere anywhere but here.

"Are you okay? Is there a problem? You're going to have to talk to me, or there would be other consequences."

The church was creepy, with a gothic eon feeling and something was wrong with the chandelier. It kept blowing and blinking; the lighting caused rooms to have a grey tint. The wind echoed with cathedral ceilings. Calvin's desk was shoved in the corner with a few odd folding chairs around the room. Calvin's voice was soft but cautionary. I didn't trust him. Fuck. What if he called my parents?

I didn't admit to anything the first time he asked. I remember thinking, "How odd, does he know something?"

The next piano class, maybe my face was too flushed, but he asked me again, this time in a stern manner.

"Rhonda, can you stay after class? I think we need to talk. I think there's a problem?"

My thoughts became defensive, but I couldn't escape his voice. I was too fucked up by now, dizzy half the time, unbalanced with a little guilt, but more fear I'd get caught. Right after purging there is about a half hour to an hour or longer when some people believe they are perfectly balanced and clear, but in reality, their cheeks are puffy, and their internal organs are trying to settle. *Ed* is creeping up on them casting a dark tunnel. I liked to compare the feeling to a "high" but a purging high is like being in orbit. Calvin could see the signs of bulimia that a non-trained person wouldn't notice.

    Every day after I got home from college, after dinner, I looked in the mirror. I began assessing my body. I was down to a tight size seven jeans. My goal was a size 2. When I ate dinner at home, I ran to my room to watch the food digest in my stomach. I was thin enough to witnesses the lump of peristalsis and watch my food move from my esophagus to my stomach. Checking the mirror, I made sure my ribs and clavicles protruded. I touched the bones and positioned so I could see them easier. I bent over backwards to see my spine.

I didn't realize the symptoms of bulimia until I began to read about purging both online and in books in the '90's. Bulimics develop a chipmunk appearance (*"chipmunk"* again) after purging and experience a "purging high" that can last for however long. Their face is oddly flushed but tiny blood vessels are visible in the cheeks. Their eyes can be bloodshot, puffy and around the orbital. The disorder is difficult to see because the signs are subtle. The one defining sign is puffy cheeks from vomiting. Then a professional should casually glance at the knuckles for chafe and redness. Though most bulimics are smart and know to use hand lotion. Their lips are puffy, or inflamed, and maybe pouty. Their voice doesn't really change but can become softer to hide the grittiness of the vomiting. They aren't necessarily skinny or underweight. They pretend things are fine, but the problem is just beginning.

To a bulimic, after a good purge, everything is perfect. She feels numb and the mood is exhilarating. Some people describe this as a post purge high. After self-induced vomiting a serotonin affect creates a good feeling that is temporary, but in truth it drastically decreases the serotonin in the body. The decrease causes a high feeling. And the process repeats. This would be considered the purging high.

The bulimic victim keeps reaching for the purging high, then not to mention the scales and clothing size. In a perfect circle, self-induced vomiting impersonates as beauty and perfection even though the bulimic victim (this happens to men, but more often girls and women) knows it's wrong and is filled with guilt. They have to throw up because bulimia makes them think they need to get rid of the food. A couple of months into the purging cycle, and it becomes a disorder really quick.

Calvin kept asking me, stern but soft, after class until I was forced to answer one time, "What the hell is wrong with you?"
He kept *nagging* and I blurted out to him.

"I do this thing," I said in a meek tone. "I make myself puke with my fingers you know, oh it's so gross. Haha, I'm so embarrassed. So, you know, I don't gain weight."

He asked, "What are you trying to say? Are you purging food, self-induced vomiting?"

"Yeah, I guess" I said. My face flushed with embarrassment.

He said, "You're not supposed to be doing that. How long have you been doing that? It's going to become a disorder and you are going to make yourself sick." His voice was beginning to rise.

I said, "How did you know I was doing that?"

He said, "Your eyes are red. Your cheeks are red, and it's not cold outside. You look like a druggy, but you don't do drugs, least I don't think you do." He said. "You're skinny and I think you're getting skinnier. I could tell something wasn't right. Maybe you need to get checked out at the University Clinic."

"I don't need a clinic," I spat back.

"The clinic, to get your labs checked," he said.

"How do you know so much about this?" I asked.

"Last year I attended a conference for teachers regarding girls with eating disorders. That's what you have. We learned if the behavior goes over a month, it can be deadly. Eventually it will kill you. Do you realize what you're doing?" He said.

I said, "No. I've not read anything about it. I learned about how to stay thin in El Dorado in the summer from 2 girls in a bathroom. They told me how."

He said, "You're not skinny just from *that*, damn. How much do you *eat*?" His voice was raising in a feared manner.

I said softly with a frown, "I eat a turkey sandwich, apple, chips, Tab and dinner at home."
He said, "I don't think so."

He sighed and rolled his eyes. He said, "Sweetie, you are on the brink of having full blown anorexia and bulimia. I care about you. It's my responsibility. You're my student. If you keep doing this, you'll get really sick. You can get help before it gets worse."

I didn't know what to say. I was ashamed and guilty.

I said, "I'll think about it. I promise I won't do it again, because you have me scared."

He gave me a hug, and as I left, he said, "You're going to get worse. You need help."

Every Wednesday and Friday in November, I hung around after class, "How are you doing? I can see what you are doing. I knew you'd not stop. You need help, sweetie, have you started eating more? Food causes you to live. It won't kill you." He said.

I said, "I can't afford help. I don't know what to do. Besides, I'm not sick or disordered or whatever it is."

He said, "We've got to find out why you're doing this. Did anyone in your family have eating disorders?"

"I have no idea," I answered, "I was adopted."

He sighed, and said, "Girls with eating disorders don't just choose to have them, they are born with them. You know, like homosexuals? They don't choose to be that way. I have students who are torn up inside because of their sexuality. You do know that homosexuals are born that way, right?"

"Of course, they don't have a choice," I said.

I stared at him blank. He can't be gay, no way, why did he ask? Maybe he's just comparing. Frankly, I didn't care if someone was homosexual or not, nor did I care if Calvin was gay. It really didn't matter. I never thought about it. I knew that's how they were born with no choice so whatever. I knew a lot of gay guys at the university.

He explained, "Like manic depression it can run in families, I know you know what that is, you're in a mental health class."

Sure, I did, I excelled in the mental disorders class of my music therapy training. Eating disorders wasn't in the curriculum.

I said, "Oh… Why are you interested in eating disorders?"

He responded after a pause, "This is fucked up. Oh sorry, my language. My little sister died of anorexia last year. She starved herself. She was 17. So, I attended a weeklong conference for professionals about eating disorders in San Francisco. And I made a promise to help anyone I noticed that might have problems. I think you are beyond problems. I think you're sick"

I asked I think trying to break up the subject, "Do you have a girlfriend? Did she break up with you after your sister died?"

He said, "No I don't have a girlfriend. No, I'm not dating anyone. No, I'm not gay. I'm too busy with teaching piano to have a girlfriend."

I said cheerfully, "I'm scales motivated. Can you believe I still wear a 9, and weigh 118? Damn Calvin. I hate my fucking scales. I wish I could kick the god damned thing across the room." At this point, watching my language wasn't an option and I didn't care what I said.

Calvin said. "Sometimes eating disorders are hereditary. I can't help treat you, I don't know how. But

I do know the facts. You are one of my favorite students. I'd hate for something to happen to you."

Could I have an eating disorder? I'd been obsessing over calories since, uh oh. I knew was headed for trouble and I couldn't stop.

Chapter 29

A SLIVER OF APPLE PIE

One Saturday in late November of 1980 after the horrifying election, Lester visited from Utah. November was beautiful in Savannah but a little cold. The weather wasn't predictable. The trees still had the look of fall, and the hills were orange, brown and even a little green peeked through the trees. Wind was changing from warm southern air to cold northern air. Soon it would be time for pumpkin pie, hot chocolate and Thanksgiving.

Lester's mom baked an apple pie. It was a sweet gesture. Making an apple pie was a lot of work. Lester added a note taped to the bottom of the pan, "I miss you."

I missed Lester. I spent hours planning meals and doing homework, neglecting my personal life. I was still trying to figure out how people cut carbs, the newest gimmick. It wasn't carbs that mattered, it was calories, so I had to preplan how many calories I was planning on eating.

I bought a different calorie counting book at the university bookstore. It was mammoth in size. I started checking every food I ate. I continued to note the calories of food, and still divided the servings down to one piece in my notebook. I took a quick glance at the calories in a piece of apple pie.

A piece of apple pie had 496 calories. Well, shit, that was enough calories for one day. I rounded the calories to 500, divided it by four, the answer being 125 calories, which was just a sliver.

I served him a piece of pie. Then cut a piece in quarters. I put the piece of pie on my plate.

Lester said, "You're eating a sliver of pie."

I said, "Calories, you know?"

"Calories?" said Lester.

"496 or 500 in a piece of homemade pie," I said, "that's too many. I already ate lunch and I have to eat dinner."

I was slick at lying about the amount of food I actually ate, vs the meals served.

"Oh." said Lester. "I guess with a dance class you do need to worry about how much you eat."

I aced it again! I often used dance class as an excuse not to eat and it worked every time.

Lester and I hugged, and he left. His dad's milk company was growing. Grocery stores were making orders, even my mom mentioned seeing it in the milk aisle.

I added the calories of cake, cookies, hamburger buns, turkey, chicken, pizza and divided the servings to one. If I ate a 1/2 cup of rice per serving, was it cooked, or uncooked? Mexican restaurants triple the amount of rice so how could a person figure the exact amount in a serving? Was I supposed to carry a measuring cup? After buying the new calorie counting book, food became more complicated and mathematical. I shouldn't have skipped algebra.

Weekend dinners weren't complicated as long as I eyeballed my servings and measured my portions. I set a calorie goal of 500 which was only a tiny amount of food considering a Snicker bar is 250, and an apple is 95.

I started writing down everything I ate. Though I kept a notebook of the calories in foods, I hadn't started noting my meals. This made it easier to hit 500. I felt better but gained a few pounds increasing my jeans size to eleven. I continued to do 50 crunches a day, increasing them to 75. They hurt my coccyx on the hard floor. I complained to my mom, "Mom, the exercises hurt my butt." We bought an exercise mat. Packaged with the mat was a booklet of primitive drawn exercises for the "woman at home."

Every calorie and exercise book I bought, or read, published in 1980 was for the "woman with no time to go to the gym." They had line illustrations and poor instructions.

I had to read a booklet of instructions for the exercises on the new mat. I started increasing my crunches to 100 a day, adding plies and leg lifts. The exercise books didn't mention cardio, most were filled with yoga or Pilates. The exercises were called "calisthenics" and I hated them.

On Monday I had a test in English Composition which I passed. I always did well in the class as long as I studied and did the homework. It was also piano day, but I didn't hang around after class. Calvin just stared at me.

Tuesday, I had music theory. Wednesday, I stayed after piano class, being proud I started exercises at home. I insisted I was eating a little more, He was unimpressed.

"You do know that girls with anorexia exercise constantly?" he said, "You need help. Here's a number, call it. You don't have to pay if you can't. You pay by sliding scale. I don't know anyone else around here that can provide the help you need, in fact, I doubt that Community Mental Health have the correct therapist. Even in St. Jose or Kansas City, I can't think of anyone and that is too far to drive from here. A fact, once the pattern of anorexia or bulimia is set, it never leaves, there is no cure, like manic depression that I talked about last week. Eating disorders are a mental problem you are often born with. Since you don't know your history, I'm suspecting someone in your biological family had the same problem. As for therapists, I don't know of anybody off hand who understands. But give them a try. The kind of help you need hasn't reached the Midwest, it's popular in California. But call them anyway, just to set my mind at ease." I took the business card and crumbled them up in my tight size 11 jeans. (The mother fuckers, I couldn't get back down to a size 7.)

The phone number was the Community Mental Health Organization in Savannah, who charged per income. I didn't have any income and the visits were free.

I kept the business card in my backpack and used it as a bookmark in the calorie counting book. Calvin asked me on Friday, "Have you called yet?"

I called the number after about a week of staring at the business card. Maybe I did need help, but I didn't want to turn loose of what I had., what if I gained weight? I already was gaining weight.

When I began classes at Northwest University, I weighed 130. I now weighed 123, up two pounds after setting a calorie goal at 500 a day. For woman 5 foot 1 inches tall, 130 is one notch from being obese on the BMI charts. To me, that made me fat. No way had I developed the problems Calvin told me about. Maybe someone would guide me in nutrition at the Mental Health Community Center. I called the number.

    I told my mom I was going to the library. I walked to the library and Savannah Square a lot. The Mental Health Community Center was located on Savannah Square. The Mental Health Community Center was the only active business left on the square. I phoned the front desk, requesting a male therapist. They assured me I'd have a male. My social skills were so poor that telling any stranger the truth about my eating habits would be difficult.

Chapter 30

HIGH ANXIETY

I entered the front doors of the Mental Health Community Center. Inside was a row of doors, offices and a waiting room where elderly people sat reading magazines or books. Some of the clients were dirty and I thought they were homeless. The clients never acknowledged anyone in fact, most, kept their eyes focused on a magazine. Some wore dirty clothes. Some didn't comb their hair, and some clients smelled of old body odor. It was the worse population, unclean and filthy.

I was told my assigned therapist name, Edith.

"You said I'd have a male therapist," I said.

"Well, we gave you a female. Please sit down and fill out your demographics," The woman at the desk said.

I immediately didn't care for Edith. I doubt she ever dealt with anyone who had an eating disorder. She was an older woman, tall with grey hair and glasses. She wore her hair in a bun, like a schoolteacher. She wore grey polyester pants, and a silk shirt, tucked in properly. Her face had a smirk of an uncaring expression, and her voice was all business. I think I could see an adult incontinent product under her grey pants which seemed tight. Occasionally I'd get a waft of urine smell.

Edith's office was nondescript, a cheap desk, with a dial phone. Everyone I knew had a push button phone. Stacked on the desk was an outdated DSM III, a book about depression, a pediatrics mental disorder book and *Firestarter* by Stephen King.

Progress notes were piled on one side of her desk in a file folder. I could read other patient's documentation. The chair in her office hurt my butt and the office was cold.

I was always cold. Being cold is a symptom of anorexia. I looked closely at the books, scanning for one about anorexia and found nothing. It should've been a red flag.

The first visit she took my history.

"Hmmm mmm. What are your symptoms?" She asked.

"Well," I said, "I might have an eating disorder. I think I do, but I don't know"

"Oh?" she said.

"Yeah," I answered, sheepishly.

"Oh. Well, I doubt it," she said. I could tell she hadn't a clue.

"Well, I eat about 500 calories a day." I hadn't purged for a couple of weeks.

"How long have you been eating 500 calories?' She rolled her eyes when I told her my symptoms.

I finally told her "I also throw up my food."

I didn't want to mess with her yet, then I started to say exactly what she wanted to hear. In mental health class, I learned how patients manipulate therapists, and I thought this was kind of fun.

I downplayed my symptoms. She didn't care.

"Well, that's not a problem, I'd call that a diet. Let's see…I'll give you an assignment and you bring it back to me next week. We'll probably have 3 sessions, and you'll be cured."

Cured was my clue. Calvin said you can't be cured of an eating disorder. I decided to play her. She needed her therapist's license revoked, if a license even existed.

She assigned me a week of exercises. One was to write down everything I ate without the calories. She said, "This exercise will help you be more aware of what you eat, and how many calories you consume per day without being aware of the amount." She had no idea I memorized calories.

The assignment reminded me of something a doctor would give an obese patient. Edith did the opposite of how she should've handled my problem.

"The other assignment is for you to write down when you, uh, throw up and note your daily weight. Don't skip weighing daily. You might have a gastrointestinal problem if you're throwing up that often. I don't deal with patients with stomach problems." She said, clueless. NO way did she believe I made myself puke.

Then she said with a pleasant close, "Come back next week. I'll read what you wrote and send you home with more assignments."

My "assignment" from the first week read like this. I was "cured" by day 3. Miraculous!

Day one: Breakfast: Biscuits

          Lunch: Cheeseburger plain

Dinner: steak with broccoli

Snack: cupcake

Throw up: I didn't.

Weight: 125.

Day two:

Breakfast: sausage biscuit from McDonalds

Lunch: pizza- 2 pieces

Dinner: 3 tacos

Snack: bag of Twizzlers

Didn't throw up.

Weight: 126

Day three:

Breakfast: Sausage biscuit. (I got more creative on day three.)

Lunch: Cheeseburger plain and fries

Dinner: Steak and baked potato

Snack: Apple pie with iced cream

Throw up: I don't do that anymore. (Yay!)

Weight: 125

Day four:

Breakfast: Pancakes with maple syrup

Lunch Turkey sandwich, potato chips, apple

Dinner: cheeseburger plain, fries

Throw up: No

Weight: 125.5

I couldn't raise my daily weight too high on the form. She was so dumb though; she'd believe I gained ten pounds.

My daily food list got creative, and my food choices read like a perfect day, possibly more food than the average person eats. My weight, by the paper, was increasing. But the truth, it stayed around 125, then decreased by force. I hated weighing 125. I kept trying to maintain my calories at 500, but sometimes I would eat 800 calories a day. Gaining weight was a nightmare. There were times when I weighed myself that if the scales didn't go down, I literally would be tempted to grab the razor to my wrist. No more of this bullshit.

I started maintaining a constant pattern dieting at 500 calories a day. A couple of days I went over 500, ate cake at lunch and purged. I finally lost a couple of pounds.

I visited my therapist, week 2, and handed her the assignment. I lost 3 pounds, and was happy with my success, but on paper, I gained 2 pounds. It was nice outside, a warm fall week for November. I liked that I walked to the therapist. I had drunk a quart of water if she offered to weigh me. (Drinking water before a doctor's appointment is called "water-logging". It causes water weight and manipulates the scale. I knew nothing about waterlogging, didn't learn it from anyone.)

She read my worksheet and was pleased.

"Are you still throwing up?" She asked.

She didn't give a shit about me. She wasn't getting paid, so why bother go listen?

I answered, "Of course not. That is a disgusting habit. I've had so much help from you that I stopped throwing up the day after I began writing down my food. See, in my notebook." I called it *habit* on purpose.

She looked over her glasses and said, "I can tell you're gaining so much weight, your face looks full. I think next week is your last visit. You're doing good, I thought as soon as I met you, I could help you and free you from your habits and find the cure! I've had great luck curing people of their anxiety and I knew I could cure you."

"Anxiety? Huh?" I thought, "Did I just hear her say that?"

My face looked *puffy*. ("chipmunk") I bet she thought, "I am going to break you of your habits." She acted like she was about to point her finger at me. I was her win and victory.

This was a big red fucking flag. Cured *of anxiety*? Have you read anything about eating disorders?

I decided to manipulate her another week, just for fun.

"You'll have one more visit. I don't think you need three like I said at first. Let's continue your assignment, this time I'm giving you a brochure on manic depression and anxiety, plus a nice workbook to fill out. You'll turn the workbook into me at your next visit," she said.

"I never said I had anxiety. I think I have an eating disorder," I said.

"It's anxiety that causes you to turn against food. I thought of you last week and realized that you have an extreme amount of clinical anxiety," she said.

The workbook consisted of questions about anxiety and what caused it. I was to fill in the blanks for five days.

1. Did I feel anxiety?

2. What do I think started the anxiety?

3. What did I do to stop the anxiety?

4. Name something good about today?

I filled out the workbook making it appear that I was completely cured of my problems with anxiety by Edith. All the anxiety she caused made my eating disorder worse.

I visited Edith one last time and turned in my workbook. She declared me cured and gave me a business card.

Chapter 31

Thanksgiving

It was tiring eating 500 calories a day. I began the pattern of purging two days a week. *Well, at least not three,* I thought. I changed the time of my lunch to Calvin's free time. I could eat, then purge, I assured him the therapist was helping me, even after I stopped seeing her. I *even* lied to Calvin.

  To an anorexic patient Thanksgiving is a nightmare. The holiday scared me. I found out that Calvin was spending Thanksgiving alone, and I invited him to eat with my family. There was always extra food; I couldn't stand anyone spending Thanksgiving alone. Of course, he declined.

Thanksgiving went smooth. I filled my plate to about 700 calories, and everything was delicious.

After I helped my mom clean the kitchen, we watched football with my dad. I loved watching football with my dad. Another Thanksgiving tradition was watching the Kansas City Plaza Light Ceremony on Maryville's news channel. They reported from Kansas City.

Mom said, "We're going to go to Kansas City and watch the Plaza lights one year."

Dad said, "Why would you want to go to Kansas City? Look at the crowd." The number of people standing watching the lights was astounding. I often wondered if that many people actually lived in Kansas City, or did they travel to watch the lights?

I had a month of classes left for first semester of college. Calvin would no longer be my instructor. He only taught piano 101. With me moving my lunch to his break time, I didn't talk to him as much. It was a poor decision. But I needed to study my English and had a thesis paper due. I wrote it on religion but had no idea what a thesis statement was or how to construct one.

One day in class he said, "Did you decide to go back to algebra?"

I said, "No, I needed to change my lunch time so I could study English in the library. I flunked algebra"

Chapter 32

JOHN LENNON

On December 8th of 1980, John Lennon was shot. I felt like I was in a different world. It changed life. It was a humid cold day in Savannah. I remember the sun being out, but the clouds were grey.

I began to behave strange. My breakfast and lunch consisted of a can of Tab. I didn't care if I ate anything or not. So, I didn't. I ate very little at dinner. If I ate more than I thought I needed, I went to the private bathroom at home to purge.

I discovered I could go to the private bathroom at home and purge without being caught. Vomiting in the bathroom at home was faster than college, but it has its drawbacks, mainly, plumbing. I ran lukewarm water for noise. I lifted the toilet lid, squatted on the floor, quickly propelled both my index finger and middle finger of my down my throat, tickled the entrance to my esophagus and out came the undigested food. I washed my face, spit out water, flushed the toilet twice, and came back to the table.

    Worked like a charm. I only did this when I ate too much. Redness and chaffing were developing on my knuckles. My fingernails were short from biting. Sometimes self-induced vomiting stung my nails. After, I always checked to make sure my stomach was flat.

    I started doing 200 crunches. I ran my hand down my ribs afterwards.

One day at lunch at the university, I was in the breakroom in the basement of the Fine Arts building. I overheard some dancers talk of "Chew and Spit." The dancers sat straddled in chairs. I never figured out why dancers sat like this. Each one would grab the chair, turn it around, and straddle it. They never sat still. They always drank soda or ate standing up. They moved like snakes. Their motions were like watching a weird dance.

"Did you ever chew and spit, instead of restrict or eat and purge?" The dancer said while twisting around in the chair. No conversation was off limits in the small break room.

"Yeah, I think Jimmy does that," the other girl said.

The first girl said, "Well he's always skinny, perfect body. How do you do it?"

"You know, you spit your food out in your napkin instead of swallow it. Jimmy's really good at it. It works but it's kind of gross. It's grosser than barfing." The first girl said in a sexy tone.

I didn't start practicing chew and spit immediately. It seemed disgusting and way worse than barfing.

The holidays, Christmas and New Year's, were a fast whirl. It didn't snow but was a bitter cold. Winter wasn't pretty to me, it was grey, and coats, hats and layers were an extra baggage. Besides I was constantly shivering. Nothing could keep me warm.

I had bulimia, possibly anorexia, and knew it. My school schedule changed. My lunch time changed. I felt alone. I felt sick.

Bulimia was grotesque and embarrassing. This is why I kept it secret. It is the dirtiest secret, I believe, a female or male could keep. The damage to the neurotransmitters could be permanent. It depletes serotonin, dopamine and norepinephrine. This causes the affected person to create an addiction. The act of self-induced vomiting causes constant reuptake of neurotransmitters to the point of depletion.

Bulimia is worse than heroin to stop. There's no addictive poison going into the body. Bulimia's a signal inside the head. It affects the hypothalamus. I hadn't a clue that throwing up food could kill you. I vomited weekly, if not daily. I started distancing myself from people while I created a covert sickness.

One afternoon, I visited the pizza buffet, near my house, alone. The pizza buffet had a single bathroom with a lock on the door. After eating a plate of 2 slices, I would sneak to the bathroom. I waited a few minutes for the pizza to hit my stomach and stuck my fingers down my throat three times. This would bring up the pizza I had previously eaten; therefore, not causing any of it to hit my fat thighs. I would eat another plate, and drive home. I would go to the bathroom and repeat. Pizza was drier and hard and painful to force up. A lot of times it caused so much pain and I had to lay down afterward.

Chapter 33

LAXIES

While hanging around the dancers, I learned about laxative abuse. Laxative abuse isn't pretty. It's worse than self-induced vomiting. It causes weight gain, bloating, screws with electrolytes and can lead to irritable bowel syndrome, rectal hemorrhoids, rectal protrusion, rectal cancer, rectal fissures, colon cancer, diabetes, heart failure, death.

    I turned 19, desperate for thin thighs. I weighed around 123. I went to the grocery store and included a box of Ex-lax in my cart. Instead of the usual weekly trip to the bathroom after eating at the pizza buffet, I ingested 4 Ex-lax. I thought this was the answer.

Ex-lax tasted like sweet medicine with a candy coating. I took Ex-lax for women, which was a lighter dose. The instructions were to ingest up to 2, every 6 hours, no more than 4 in a 24-hour time

I went to the university library and learned everything I could about which type of laxatives existed from the Physician Desk Reference on the shelf. I learned about what each laxative did and how they acted. Ex-lax is a stimulant laxative, such as Dulcolax and Senokot. The action is a stimulation of the bowel tract to speed up bowel movements through the lining of the intestines. It takes about 12 hours. Taking 4 at a time doesn't speed up the mechanism. It makes the action painful due to the speed and intensity of the bowel movement. Taking 4 at a time causes a faint feeling after. It isn't the smartest way to get rid of food. I took 4 at a time, never more. In some books I have read of women ingesting the whole box.

    The effects weren't immediate, hitting me while in the car driving to college the next morning. I tried timing it at 12 hours. By the time I got to college, parked, my stomach looked like I was 6 months pregnant. I ran to a bathroom and had a butt explosion literally filling the toilet until I crapped out water. My god, and I was okay with it. I felt drained yet successful. My entire stomach contents flushed, and probably every electrolyte in my body as well. I used the bathroom countless of times. My stomach was flat, and I noticed my thighs were beginning to thin. I was mad because I couldn't weigh myself after my rectum had the grand explosive bowel movement.

I didn't really care for the laxatives, but took them on a weekly basis, if I ate. If I ate pizza, I would either purge at the restaurant, or consume 4 Ex-lax later. I watched my weight go down to 122, then 120. Almost back to 118.

Between class breaks, I visited the bookstore. I glanced up and down the aisles in search of something, anything on anorexia or bulimia. It wasn't until I found both *Starving for Attention* in 1982 and in 1986, I bought a book about an anorexic ballerina, called, "*Dancing on my Grave*". They spoke of chew and spit, laxative use and restricting along with the extreme exercising of a ballerina. I guess I was ahead of my time.

My weird behaviors were becoming frequent, as Calvin had predicted. Laxative abuse, 2 times a week, purging after regular meals daily and restricting calories became my life.

Chapter 34

TRIGGERS

In my notebook I wrote a list with "safe" and "unsafe" foods. If I ate anything on the list, I purged immediately.

I finished mental health clinical in music therapy. I learned that patients often trick the therapist. I did the same with Edit, but she was dumb.

I finally weighed 118 and continued to weigh myself every day. My goal was 95.

As my behavior worsened, I felt weak. Every time I saw a dancer's ribs, thighs or clavicles, I stared, my brain could feel the triggers start. Once while I was eating lunch (peanut butter crackers, Tab) in the break room at college, a male dancer told another male dancer in an effeminate voice, "You're getting flabby, that's not sexy." The other guy said, "Honey, I know just what to do about it." The other guy said, "Now that is sexy." I knew what they were talking about.

My mind wandered, "what would *he* do about it? Guys don't do that; this is a girl's disease."

I went to bed starving but ignored it. Hunger was useful, and a great way to lose weight. This is proven but is supposed to be useful when a person has an "Obese" BMI. It is not useful nor suggested if a person has a BMI of 19, and a BMI of 19 is almost at the overweight line in the chart.

If I felt my blood sugar drop, I'd eat a few Skittles. One or 2 Skittles were fine, as each one is 4 calories. If I got to feeling faint, I'd go to the dining area and eat an apple, carefully watching my weight each day. I knew the trick to a successful anorexic day was to eat enough so I'd never binge. And it worked. I never binged, and kept my weight around 118-120, with my preconceived notion that my thighs were huge.

Chapter 35

I FIRST MET DEAN

I had already read Jack Kerouac when I was sixteen. I had aspirations at 19 to trace his footsteps.

    I planned a trip to both New York City and New Orleans, because Jack Kerouac visited both cities. While I read Jack Kerouac, I got lost in his travels with his buddies and adventures. His buddies and adventures made me thrive, if there was anything left of me. I became a young fan of everything Jack Kerouac wrote. Any time I traveled I visited where he went, and took a few minutes to breath, pause and be gracious.

In 1981, I decided to write him a fan letter. This was a failure after I went to the library to look up his birth date, and then found his death date in 1969.

I visited a travel agent at a local mall. That was the only way to plan trips and vacations in 1981. The agent had a book on New York City that was priced $15.95. It was full of colorful enticing pictures of Central Park, Times square, Wall Street Financial District, Soho, Bryants Park, Twin Towers, Statue of Liberty. He gave it to me. I read the travel book daily. I planned which hotel I'd stay in, and what I'd do. I didn't know about manifesting in 1981. I'd read for hours, forgetting to eat.

I practiced my violin and stared at my little wrist. I could circle the knuckle of my index finger to my thumb around it. I had tiny wrists and ankles. My butt hurt to do my required 200 crunches. And my stomach wasn't quite as flat as it should be, due to laxative abuse. My muscles hurt, but I continued.

My music therapy class visited the Glore Psychiatric Museum in St. Joseph, Missouri. It was the highlight of my year. It was a place I forgot my problems. I could see real things, like the aquarium of stomach contents that a past patient ate from pica disorder. (Nails, tacks, etc). I learned about torture used on people with mental illnesses in the Middle Ages. The museum had examples of medical instruments used in a lobotomy. Then the bus toured a little around St. Joseph and back to the University for lunch and afternoon classes.

In the spring of 1981, the orchestra traveled to a sleek resort. I found the cleaning lady's liquor in their utility closet. I didn't like to drink. The only substance I took was laxatives. Our orchestra played well that evening, and the trip was unforgettable. The resort was exquisite, the drinking, heavy. Most of us were still drunk when we got off the bus.

As second semester ended, I got disinterested in music therapy as a career. I had a feeling it wasn't a lucrative avenue. I didn't enjoy the university atmosphere or the students. I hated lunch. I couldn't approach anyone and had only a few friends. As skinny as I was, they thought I was using drugs. I wanted to major in dance or journalism and did neither. I didn't like to play music; I didn't even like to hear it in my car. The only friend I had was Jeremy.

I really wanted to be a writer. And after writing my thesis paper on religion, I could be a chaplain or a clergy of a Buddhist temple (not knowing the path of this career, the correct term is llama. Jack Kerouac was a devout Buddhist. I intended to follow him.). But I didn't choose those lines of work or classes. I knew I didn't want to be a musician and not a music therapist. I told my parents.

They understood. I didn't return to class the third year. Had I returned, I would've majored in journalism.

Chapter 36

AFTER COLLEGE

After college, I didn't know what I wanted to do for a career. I started looking for a real job. I still kept my meals to a minimum of 500 calories, but without Tab or cheese and peanut butter crackers, I didn't know what to eat. I finally bought both out of desperation. My mom said, "I don't know what to do with you," and rolled her eyes.

    In my quiet time I would continue to read, or cross stitch. I was already interested in quilting but only knew to cut and sew fabric together. While I was home, my habits were controlled. I felt off-track. I tried to maintain my college diet: Tab, cheese peanut butter crackers. It was hellacious. My family noticed. Mom would try to get me to eat cookies, but I knew cookies had over 100 calories a piece. I was a mess.

While at a bookstore in Maryville, I bought the book, *Starving for Attention* by Cherry Boone. It's still available and not the best book for someone with an eating disorder.

Starving For Attention is an autobiography about a celebrity's eating disorder. I read it and reread it. I learned more tricks and became fluent at restricting calories. The book opened up a whole new avenue. I knew I had bulimia the book made it official. It was the one of only books written about anorexia at the time.

The first 6 months out of college, I managed to get a job. It was miserable. It was at a fast-food restaurant. While at work, I wore black t-shirts under my uniform. I wore thick eye liner.

I would buy laxatives, or diet pills at the drug store. I found Dexatrim on the shelves. My thighs which *were* getting fatter, needed to be thinner. Maybe over the counter diet pills would make restricting calories easier? I had a hard time sticking to 500 calories and working fast food. I went to the local bookstore and found more books about eating disorders. I kept my job for quite a while. I always worked so I could have my own money. But my food bondage was becoming something I couldn't control.

I weighed about 120. It was 1982. I quit working fast food and started working at a day care. It was a fun job. I enjoyed the children's activities. I thought the day care director seemed suspicious of me, never knew why. Could it be that I hardly ate anything? Once she pulled me aside and asked, 'Is there anything you need to tell me?" That was weird, almost in my personal space.

A few things, body wise began to change. When I took laxatives, their effect started to become sluggish. I found I needed more just to evacuate my bowels. I felt nauseous when taking them. They were messing with my metabolism, and I felt constantly felt sick. I would try to throw up but that also wasn't working. I took a break from everything: Purging, laxatives, caloric counting and gained 4 pounds fast. I stopped food obsessions for the time being. I began to get puffy looking in my face. I could almost see my clavicles disappear. My ribs weren't protruding as I thought they should. I stopped doing crunches cause of the pain in my butt. It wasn't a good sign when I stopped obsessing over food and weight. I gained weight so fast; it was hard to bring it back down to the correct number.

After weighing myself one day and discovering the gain of almost 6 pounds, I freaked out, slammed the scales down, yelled my favorite words to the scales, "You stupid mother fucker," and started restricting calories and writing down food.

I know some people who struggle and eat and eat till they gain. It doesn't matter to them, because they are not scales obsessed. My success was scales based. Failure is a gain on the scales. I was struggling not to eat, and felt it's almost the same condition as overeating.

One of my friends had an "OBESE" BMI. Let me explain OBESE BMI's: BMI under 24.9 is normal. BMI under 18.5 is underweight. BMI over 25 is overweight. BMI over 30 is obese. BMI over 40 is morbidly obese, meaning they are 40 pounds or over their ideal body weight. Most who have BMI's over 30 qualify for diet pills, but insurance doesn't cover it. Back in 1983, insurance often covered it, and prescription diet pills were easier to obtain. I weighed about 124 and obtained phentermine from my friend. My weight went back down to 120 with the diet pills, and I learned to not stop obsessing about food. This isn't the last time I learned this. The third time my weight went sky high.

Chapter 37

NEW ORLEANS

In 1983, I continued to plan my trip to New Orleans. It was easier to plan, because we had a new computer. I took to computers immediately and loved it. It was a monstrous IBM, with little memory and a huge price tag. The modem was dial up, but it was all I knew.

I "logged on" and started searching for anything New Orleans. This wasn't the internet Al Gore invented, but it started grand, in a small caliber. We had cable television, and my favorite show was Fame.

I still managed my weight with unhealthy actions. I got tired of laxatives and stopped taking them. They didn't entice me and were gross. Their taste turned into pungent instead of sweet. Their smell made me want to hurl. Their outcome, too disgusting to describe. I grew to repulse them. Even now I don't take one unless I eat so little, I can't have a bowel movement. Times have changed around laxatives, and people get colon cleansers (an expensive form of a laxative in a bottle at the health food store) or colonics, which cleans out your entire colon track, leaving the stomach perfectly flat and the scales down by several pounds. Colon cleansers are a temporary myth.

    I maintained a weight of around 120. 120 BMI was 22.7 for me. There were BMI charts all over the message boards online. I kept my weight at 120 by keeping track of what I ate, truthfully, knowing every calorie I put into my mouth, and the occasional purge.

Online, I found a darker world. Being on dial-up, I couldn't spend hours searching, but there was a world out "there" of girls exactly like myself. It wasn't called Pro ana. It was hidden behind a search, which was often left with a blank black or blue web page. Email appeared to be DOS configured, and unimportant. Message groups existed, if one was smart enough to discover them, but were hard to find.

CompuServe was the server most houses had with the privilege of having dial up modems. Dial up modems were huge and not common. There were so many cords that plugged in to the phone and the computer. The phone had to be unplugged from the cord, the cord had to be plugged into the computer. It was craziness. When I was finished on the computer, I plugged the cord back into the phone. If someone wanted to reach us while on the internet, it would signal like a fax machine. DSL modems were a pain in the butt. But they existed. And they opened up another world, temporarily, but present.

In primitive message groups, girls typed on a black and white screen, and call each other fat. Or ask if anyone had eaten, and how many crunches they did that day. Or they would ask, "My mom found my laxies, what do I do?" etc. And people would answer, and act like they cared.

"Oh, honey. Now you'll have to be extra secretive. Try to hide them in your sock drawer, then be sure to fold up your own socks." Some tips were helpful. Others, rude, "Well, you should've been more careful, bitch. I guess it's time you have to stop. Haha."

I spent evenings in my room reading travel books about NYC and New Orleans. I went back to the travel agent, and planned a trip to New Orleans by train, alone for 5 days. I asked for 5 days off at the day care where I worked and started packing.

I packed my luggage 3 times to make sure I don't forget anything. I made a list, and checked it off, handling every object 3 times each. Repack repack repack. I packed On the Road and the Dhammapada. It was time consuming and time loosing. But I needed to make sure everything was just so in my suitcase. I said "goodbye" to my dad and mom.

My mom took me to the train station in Maryville with my luggage. I waited for the train at the large, populated station, with a couple of other people. I sat down on a bench and stared at the track until I heard the whistle. The train ride took 21 hours down to New Orleans, 21 hours back. "21 hours" thought I, "No meals haha." The train arrived and I handed the attendant my ticket and boarded. I had a window seat.

The train itself was freezing. I watched out the window at every stop. There were people living in cardboard boxes. The boxes were made into houses filled with old, ragged blankets. I could see heating sources but couldn't figure out how they plugged them in. Some people had old, rusted grills lit. It was June, not cold during the day but temperatures dropped at night. The most homeless population of people living in boxes was around St. Louis, Memphis and the stops after central Missouri.

The train was titled "City of New Orleans," like the classic song. I could hear Arlo Guthrie singing the song as I rode the train. The conductor was the greatest conductor on earth. He sang into the microphone over bridges, gave facts about each city and made the trip a piece of American history. Crossing into Louisiana from Tennessee the terrain began to change. Spanish moss and green valleys started to appear from below the bridges. Magnolia trees and swamp land emerged. The land in Louisiana is really beautiful to capture in the eyes. The 21-hour train ride gave my body and mind a chance to recover slightly, from the abuse of the last few years. I felt a balance start to return.

I stayed in New Orleans for 5 days in a dirty YMCA. YMCA's were about $25 a night and both men and women could stay. The room was grey cement with a bunker type of bed. There was a chair and a desk. Nothing fancy, but it was a place to stay. I had to bug bomb my room as soon as I got there. The people who sold the bug bomb to me at Walgreen's said, "Our roaches are our friends." The roaches, most likely weren't everyone's friends in New Orleans. Some were the size of tennis balls.

At the YMCA, I was either bound for taking taxis, walking everywhere or taking a streetcar. The nearest restaurant was a streetcar stop away. I decided walking was much better. So, I chose to walk most places. (It's smarter to buy a week pass for the streetcar, instead of walking everywhere.) I walked to the original Popeye's and bought the special. It was 2 chicken strips and French fries. I paused to look at it, realized I hadn't eaten in almost 24 hours, and slowly ate it. It wasn't on my food list, but I was famished. I walked back to the YMCA and to my room. Whenever I ate anything, I always felt my stomach after to make sure it was flat. That is a habitual action often seen in girls and women who are afflicted with any sort of restrictive eating disorder.

I became smitten with the iron work architecture, and jazz music. I loved the levee area, and Port of Call restaurant. New Orleans was amazing. I ate once a day, carefully deciding which restaurant. As loyal to Jack Kerouac, I took the ferry to Algiers. I walked where Kerouac walked.

I read *On the Road* and bought *Big Sur* at the B Dalton's Bookstore on Canal Street. I visited a needlework shop and drank too many hurricanes in the French Quarter. They had roadside hurricane carts. I traveled with a tour bus in New Orleans and drank one at every stop. I drank a hurricane at Pat O'Bryant, with the souvenir glass.

After the bus dropped me off, I stumbled back to my room at the YMCA that night. Seriously, now that I think about it, the only time I didn't worry about how much food hit my stomach in the year of 1983, was the hurricane night. In the morning, I made a bee line to Walgreens for Excedrin.

The next day I took a swamp tour. The van driver's name was Jerry. He drove us around the swamp lands of Louisiana. Our group ate lunch at a Cajun café in the middle of the swamp. We traveled the swamp on an air boat, and Jerry cooked shrimp gumbo. We ate dinner on the swamp shore. I picked around the vegetables but didn't turn down the shrimp. Again, eat enough to not binge. I was wearing a short top and shorts and got a scorching sunburn.

    I spent a little time with Jerry after the swamp tour. He spoke of his life in the swampland. He made me a voodoo doll out of Spanish moss and taught me a French song.

The next morning, I took the train back to Maryville. I was sunburned. I needed a change and the feeling around the day-care center was negative. I quit and found a different job, still not knowing what I wanted to do for a career.

Chapter 38

FAT BOOK

1984-1985 I carried a small notebook, where I recorded everything, I ate. When I used up that notebook, I got another one, copied the calories of the safe and unsafe food, and kept my calories at a minimum. I preferred to use Mead Fatbooks. They were pocket sized and fit in my purse.

I found an apartment and moved in on my own. It was in the center area of Savannah. I moved my belongings into the apartment, and all my books, and my cross stitch and quilting. The apartment wasn't clean to begin with and felt dingy. The tub was gross. I got down on my hands and knees and scrubbed it clean. I read books like *Best Little Girl in the world*. Karen Carpenter died the year before by taking Syrup of Ipecac. Ipecac syrup was a horrible way to purge, and I thought of her if I ever considered it. I didn't follow Karen Carpenter but constantly contemplated about her. I loomed over the thought of using Ipecac Syrup, until I tried it.

    I had begun purging regularly, but still avoided laxatives. I restricted calories down to one meal a day, which had a positive effect on my bank account. Down the road from my apartment was a convenience store. I walked to the little store; it was a liquor store with Hustler magazines. The clerk was a graying lady with missing teeth. She wore old jeans that looked like there was a Depends undergarment beneath them, and an old blue and grey plaid flannel shirt.

I found a bottle of Syrup of Ipecac and bought it. With her husky voice, she said, "Everyone needs that in their medicine cabinet." Boy if she only knew. I put it in my medicine cabinet and pondered over it.

I overate one day. Overeating was 3 meals a day. I took the Ipecac syrup. It tasted very syrupy with a medicinal flavor. I downed a few glasses of water after drinking the bottle. It wasn't an awful flavor. What was to follow was the purge of a lifetime. It works within 15 minutes, violently, until you vomit clear liquid, then dry heaves.

It is by far the worst and most dangerous purge and the first and last time I ever played with Syrup of Ipecac. Besides it is tasting like thick syrupy medicine, the projectile vomiting into the toilet for hours scared the shit out of me. I can't understand for the life of me how anyone could ever use it to purge. It was deadly. The fear I had while throwing up involuntarily was that I could never going to stop. I thought my heart would fail.

I looked in the mirror and my skin was grey. I vomited into the nighttime hours. Anyone who even thinks of using Syrup of Ipecac, don't. It's not the way to go. The side effects of Ipecac are muscle wasting, shortness of breath, and eventually heart failure and death. Not to mention the loss of every single electrolyte in the cellular structure. The major loss of electrolytes means a trip to the emergency room for IV, but I would never go to the ER admitting what I had done. It is not pleasant and should never be used.

The good thing that came out of Syrup of Ipecac was a huge weight drop of 4 pounds. It is not worth it, and frankly, Syrup of Ipecac is insane. I was dizzy for 3 days (most likely blood pressure drop), sick and would never touch it again.

I went back to purging nearly every day and resisting meals after recovering from the Ipecac disaster. I walked every day after work. I weighed around 125. I felt fat and pudgy. I walked with women at work. But my secret life of not eating at home kept my weight down low enough, there really wasn't a need.

At work there were often cupcakes, cookies, candy, repulsive goodies bought in by other employees. I was hired as a mail deliverer. I walked for 8 hours a day 5 days a week. My feet hurt before I got home. I had to wear a dress and heels. Heels! My weight remained at 123-125. I didn't take the time to eat at work, and it was nice to be able to avoid the junk food.

That job didn't last, because I quit. I was developing planter's fasciitis, which is also hereditary in some case studies. If people want employees to stay at jobs stop making such drastic requirements.

About this time, my parents split, but they were growing apart. My dad moved to the Lake of the Ozarks, to begin the next adventure of his life. It was January 1985.

Chapter 39

FAME

1985 included Live Aid, the boomtown Rats and I Don't Like Mondays. In 1985, my favorite TV show, Fame aired their episode in May about eating disorders. I was floored and proud they tackled the subject which could be difficult to do without creating a trigger. By 1985, I was an expert about eating disorders, and STILL refused to give mine up.

The show created a flutter of a trigger, and my sickness returned. A trigger is: *An event, person, place, thing or emotion that sets the eating disorder in place.* In 1985 there weren't websites set up as triggers as there are today. A trigger is not the cause of the disorder. Triggers can *lead* to eating disorder activities.

I began skipping breakfast, then lunch. One meal a day became my mantra. I signed up for ballet, again, so I didn't have to eat. I watched everything I could on anorexia. Lifetime channel became my favorite. What I didn't like about a lot of the eating disorder movies for television were, the girl eventually died. Or the girl miraculously recovered into a perky fake woman with no lasting side effects. Hollywood makes eating disorders appear deadly or harmless with no line in between, as I've addressed earlier. Hollywood is very inaccurate. I think some of the shows were purposefully created as a trigger.

In the '80's the movies never told the truth. I bought the book *Stick Figure*, then, *Wasted*. *Wasted* was the ultimate truth. It was written in a perfect, non-glamorizing account of everything that goes on in an eating disordered patient's mind. I loved that book, and read it, reread it, and reread it again. *Wasted* wasn't fake. It was real as shit and in your face.

I started drinking tea for breakfast. I'm a tea drinker, not really syncing with the slight bitterness of coffee until Starbucks came out with the calorie ridden Frappuccino. I like plain tea, hot or cold. Tea is great, no calories, and a little bit of caffeine. It's better than diet coke (or Tab, which was starting to become hard to find in 1985).

I created kind of a career in 1984-1985 of going to rock concerts. It's easier to say who I didn't see, than who I did. Naturally, I was excited when Live Aid came around and they showed it on TV. Music came from cassettes bought at the record store. I delved into the Boomtown Rats, Queen, The Rolling Stones and Springsteen.

Already hung up on I Don't Like Mondays by the Boomtown Rats released in 1979, I chose to focus upon the worse part of the lyrics. Every time I heard the song, it made my thoughts darker. It molded my depression, eating disorders, any mental issue I had at the time. It caused my depression to sink so low, I'd think of cutting myself to the beat of the song. It would be easy. Perfect cuts in the ankles, never the wrist cause people would see. From Live Aid, my takeaway was Queen's set, and Bob Gelfdof's solo. I did cut myself a few times during this time, and a few more.

The other song I preoccupied myself with was Bohemian Rhapsody by Queen. It was released in 1975, but I started to engross entire evenings on the lyrics in 1985. It's supposed to be an operatic epic song and I turned it into the most depressing, remorseful, doldrums slash your wrist type of event. Oh, the drama!

After Live Aid was on tv, I couldn't turn away from either song, in the worst way possible. Those two songs kept playing in my head for years. I never got to see Queen or the Boomtown Rats. Not end of story of Bohemian Rhapsody, but in 1985, they molded my soul.

Otherwise for concerts, I saw Bruce Springsteen in December of 1984, on the cusp of 1985. He was touring for his Born in The USA album. Springsteen was a life changer. He involved the fans better than any artist

I've seen. His music and lyrics speak in ways no other performer has during my time. I became politically active.

Our house was a union home, always voting democrat. My dad was a union member in the Teamsters. The union was our way of life. I refused to cross picket lines and kept up with any strike news. I began to volunteer in political campaigns that won. It always gave me a good feeling when the candidate won, and I helped during the campaign. I really wanted to make a difference in someone's life, like Springsteen did with mine. But yet, I was weak from the eating disorder and depression was sinking in from the neuron's depletion. I was fucked up, but I'm not sure I wanted to be. I realize if I couldn't make a difference in my own life, I wouldn't in any others lives either. But I wanted to be grateful for something.

   The plus side to volunteering in political campaigns was the countless walking door to door. That was a win in and of itself. I met great people in the spring and summer of 1985. The minus side to volunteering in the campaign is the possibility of getting shot here in Missouri which is very republican. I could imagine knocking on the wrong door. I stopped canvassing after a lady in Savannah got abducted and murdered.

Chapter 40

IF YOU WANT TO HANG OUT

In late 1985, I decided I needed a social life that didn't involve food, absence of food, purging food, calories of food. I ventured into St. Joseph to enjoy the music. I went on my own, carrying On the Road with me.

St. Joseph was never clean. It was down in the dumps and filthy. And the roads were confusing. But there were great stores and clubs in the main part of the city, especially around Belt Highway near the mall. It had a blues beat.

I chose a bar that had a long stairwell into its space in an upstairs building overlooking Main Street.

With my book I sat at the bar stool. The bar frequently had blues bands and local bands, playing on the small stage. There was a less than desirable bathroom that existed, single stall with a lock on the door. Happy hour featured tacos, and general happy hour food.

The clientele was a beatnik society that blended with everything I was trying to be. They seemed to be starving for life and every single person in that bar could've been a Jack Kerouac or Neal Cassady. Maybe they were.

    The bar had a darkened empty area behind the main room. I noticed people go back there, and then return. I sat at the bar and ordered a beer. One of the guys sat near me, and we started a conversation. He was an artist, as were a lot of people in the same area. He introduced himself as 'Lowery." And he commented about *On the Road*. We began to sit together at a small wobbly table. The tables were big enough for 3 people. We sat at the same table every week.

As we got to know each other, I found out his apartment was around the corner, and given that we were friends by now, he said I could always crash out there, if I didn't feel like driving home.

Lowery had short dark brown hair, dark rimmed glasses wore black Gap style pants and usually a white or grey button-down shirt. He was about 5 foot 7.

We went to his apartment to get away from the smoke in the bar. His apartment was an artist's apartment with inks, a large lit easel for drawing, pens, pencils, paints, paint brushes, in storage but also laying around the table. The brushes and paints were in an alcove away from the easel. I'd never seen an artist's apartment and was impressed with all the designs, paper, and supplies. He gave me a beer, which I didn't decline.

Lowery drew all the concert promotion flyers in town. One venue on Main Street had each of his concert flyers covering the walls. We talked through the city in the early hours of morning, and he walked me back to my car, parked near his apartment. I made sure to never drink so much I couldn't drive. I enjoyed every moment I had with Lowery.

Eventually he began to notice how I played around with tacos removing and replacing the meat with lettuce at the bar. I often shoved food around on my plate to make people think I ate. Sometimes it worked. It didn't take long to notice my lack of food to mouth if one was around me at mealtime and observant.

One typical Thursday night, Lowery noticed I was playing around with my food. He said, "Instead of playing with your food, and I have noticed the bite to food ratio with you, I have something that will make you not even think about it."

I followed him to the dark room behind the bar. He asked, "Have you ever done any lines before?"

I said, "No."

He said, "No pressure, but would you like to share?"

I said, "Sure." I didn't turn down anything as long as it could be taken by mouth. I'd smoked marijuana before and taken diet pills which were amphetamine based. If something made me forget about food for 1 hour, I would indulge. I would never take anything that made me sleepy or out of control.

I watched as he took the white powder from a small plastic bag and put it on a credit card and divide the piles into thin white lines. He rolled a hundred-dollar bill and put it into his right nostril. He snorted the cocaine into his right nostril, then breathed away from the powder. He said, "Always breath away from the powder so it doesn't blow off the credit card." Then he repeated the left nostril.

He offered me 2 lines as well. I was careful not to breath on the credit card, but away from the it between lines. The first line went into my right nostril. I felt it give my nostril a funny clean but stuffy feeling. Then I felt it in my brain. Cocaine was a fast rush. I did the same with the left nostril. The feeling was stronger.

Everything about life was entirely clear at that very second. There were no thoughts, no feelings. I knew everything and every question was answered. For a temporary time, I was the person I thought I would become. I weighed 118 pounds, had a thin face, my hair which was long in perfect ringlets. My dress which was a gauze deadhead dress, and twirled as I moved, moved on its own, freely.

Hail to the cocaine! I could be the girl I wanted to be. Lowery was laughing at me. He began to talk, and we moved to our table in the bar. We started talking about nothing in particular. But I remember the lights being so real, and the air being crystal clear. The atmosphere was happy. Lowery and I talked about the sky, the town, the cars below.

We went outside and swung around a streetlamp pole and walked down the sidewalk. We were beatniks from *On the Road*. Lowery was Sal, I was Dean, well, a female version of Dean. Or maybe I was Sal's girlfriend. All I ever wanted to be was a female Jack Kerouac who wandered and drove around in all the cities and towns meeting up with people he knew. With cocaine I was able to reach this height of capacity.

Everything was undeniable. Even the damn sidewalk knew the answer. We walked for hours in the warm night. We talked and talked and joked. We laughed about fried barbecue bread. Fried barbecue bread is only funny if you're stoned. (*Fried bread is actually an Indian specialty. In 2012, I ate fried bread at a Pueblo in Taos. I don't know if they serve it barbeque style.*)

Nothing was out of bounds for cocaine conversations. We didn't even need beer when we snorted cocaine together. Beer would ruin the absoluteness of the power of the drug.

The headlights on the cars driving down the dark street were not only yellow but prisms in every metallic color. It was like we were staring at a High-Definition world. We walked together up and down the side of the road, dark and mysterious, but not to us. We had the entire night.

At Lowrey's apartment, we crashed together, after talking for hours into the morning. Lowery was the gentleman. In the morning, he offered me coffee. With cocaine you're not hungry. The aftereffects, though, are a bit off. My sinuses were painful. My nose would bleed. Headaches existed. Cocaine was too expensive for me to ever get hooked on or buy. Lowery bought it occasionally. I considered it like pot, and never did enough to get hooked. When Lowery and I did a few lines of cocaine, every moment counted, and nothing was lost. Lowery and I continued this through the fall into the winter. This would explain my constant sinus infections.

After a couple of months, I didn't see Lowery for a few weeks. The weather turned colder with ice storms, and I decided at that moment in 1985 that I'd never drive in snow or ice. Later I'd develop an irrational fear about driving on ice and snow.

Chapter 41

FEAR OF DRIVING

Winters seemed harsh, but probably it was my imagination. I hated my job but was happy to have one. I went to work and hoped I wouldn't need to drive anyone from the insurance company home in the snow. Once the snow was so bad it took me 3 hours to get home. My fear of driving in snow had to be met. I learned to put the fear behind me, but I never drive in snow or ice unless it's for my job, even now.

The winter snow had melted, and I went downtown to the bar. When I saw Lowery, I was shocked. His hair was messy, as if he'd not combed it for days, he had a beard and smelled like he hadn't bathed.

I acknowledged him, and he saw me. He looked away. I walked towards him, and he was distant. I said, "Hello." He grumbled, "Hello." Really it could've been his messy twin. We went to a table, and he said, "I got into hard drugs. I did things I shouldn't have done. I don't want to talk about it. You shouldn't be here. They busted the place the other day." He got up and left. I watched him walk down the street and disappear. I never saw him again nor did I return to the bar.

It made me sad, and I discovered when I was sad, instead of eating my way through despair, I starved. I'd lost a few pounds and was feeling good about it.

Chapter 42

DESPERATION

I changed jobs to *another* shitty life insurance company where they treated women like feeder cows. I seemed to make the rounds with the worse life insurance companies in the city. Both life insurance companies are out of business. The later company, the boss got arrested for embezzlement.

With the change came new stress, like waiting a month before I got a new paycheck, etc. I easily skipped meals and started walking with the ladies at work. I worked in the filing department. For hours I filed. The room was huge, and I had to go from row to row putting yellow receipts in files.

I tried to fit in with the people at that job but felt a little left out. Most were kind. But no one wanted to make contact. I knew insurance filing department wouldn't be my career, in fact, I was embarrassed to say what department I worked. The job didn't last very long.

I gained a few pounds. I was getting tired of counting food. My drive was slowing, again. For lunch I bought anything from a little rice to cheese and peanut butter crackers and got a diet coke. Employees commented, 'Hell, girl, that's not enough to feed a goddamned bird." Why anyone would pay attention to what anyone else ate is confusing to me. Does it matter? I became a little defensive.

While training a new employee who obviously was very skinny and wore skinny clothes to show it off, she looked at me and said, 'I'll never do anything to my body to lose my shape. Don't you work out or anything? You need to." I felt appalled and embarrassed. Was I getting fat? I had gained about 5 pounds. It sent me back to my bad habits and set off another round of bulimia and anorexia.

I was still taking ballet once a week and skipping meals when I had a class. I started skipping most meals except for what the employees saw me eat. I lost 3 pounds quick and wore tighter clothing. I didn't like to emphasize my shape, and felt my clothes at least were conservative for an office. My lunches turned into walks around the building. If I took enough steps, I'd not have to exercise later. I increased my crunches from 200 a day to 400 a day. It hurt to do 400 crunches. My tail bone was starting to callus.

I briefly stopped purging but started counting every calorie I put into my mouth. And this is when I perfected chew and spit. Chew and Spit was what the dancers taught me in college. It would pay off now.

My lunches, if I packed one, would be small with tons of napkins. I chose to sit by myself, so no one could see. In my corner, I would take a hefty bite of food, chew it for a while, and spit it into a napkin. It looked like I was eating.

I began to sit with other ladies, and found I could play around with my food, and act like I wiped my face with a napkin. Guess where the chewed food went? It was easy to have full conversations, half of it with the napkin in my face. No one thought anything. I could also act like I was blowing my nose, and spit into the napkin.

There was so much I could do with this skill that I learned in college!

The dangers of chew and spit are this: dental carries from too much sugar. The nutrients of the food are lost. It is equally as bad as the purge. Mouth ulcers from the acid in the stomach before swallowing the food are common and painful. Jaw pain is also common. (Muhlheim, 2016)

Weight gain is a side effect of chew and spit cause the body reacts to the smell and taste of the food and releases insulin. The release of insulin causes weight gain. The excess insulin produces hunger which is a nightmare to someone who has an eating disorder. Chew and spit should never become a habit. It can result in hyper-insulinemia. (another "mia") This is the producing of too much insulin. Too much insulin leads to insulin resistance, which causes a metabolic disorder leading to diabetes. (scienceofeds.org, 2016)

It is so gross to spit out chewed up food. It's easier to have anorexia than to use chew and spit techniques. Plus, it's too expensive to waste food. It's a huge waste of food to chew and spit it out. Chew and spit is still not considered an eating disorder in DSM V.

I discovered which food was the easiest to chew and spit and not be noticed: white rice. I began to pack only white rice for lunch. I bought the cheapest brand, because I was just going to spit it out. It worked for a long time. I lost some of the weight I gained. At home, I didn't eat a thing.

I did this for a few months. On weekends, sometimes I ate pretty well, cheeseburger, French fires. One meal a day was better than nothing.

My single meals were cheeseburgers, brats, sometimes pasta, what a normal person ate. Calorie ridden, but I walked everywhere and worked it off. I walked so much I grew to hate exercise.

But my drive continued. No way was I going to let my body become puffy. In the bathroom mirror both at work and at home, I made sure my clavicles showed, and my ribs protruded.

I counted calories, it seems for fifty years. It was the only food control I could manage.

Chapter 43

MANIC

My job at the life insurance company was filled with the doldrums. I did not like the people I worked with. I didn't like the job. I was treated like shit by both upper management and employees. Eventually the company closed, and the owner got caught embezzling.

I read Kerouac and continued on one meal a day. I was only eating once a day, so I didn't log in my food in my notebook. I weighed myself weekly. I would stop this behavior, but had to start again, because of the jump in number on the scales. I was surprised to see a rise on the scales, from 120, to 124, to 125. Then to 127 which was too much for me to weigh. I was tired of walking everywhere, logging food, scales and I stopped one day.

1986.

Burn out.

I stopped.

I couldn't do aerobic exercise. My body was sick and tired of any more exercise, and it refused to allow me to do it.

In 1986, I decided to make quilts, with patterns. My mom got me a used Husqvarna sewing machine. I sewed a log cabin quilt, a beginning primitive effort. I hadn't a clue about sewing a quilt. I managed to sew a complete stitch through my thumb and ended up at the ER.

My thumb got treated and I received a tetanus shot plus an order for antibiotics. I visited my mom's and gave her a complete visualization of my accident with the sewing machine, repeating the situation about five times. Sewing a stitch through my thumb is never anything I'd want to see in a medical chart.

I couldn't get the machine to work well but ended up with a half assed thing that resembled a quilt. My choice of batting was the cheapest on the market. There was so much polyester in the batting it made my skin itch. In the end, my dog at my mom's ended up with a new blanket.

There were a few other times I was clumsy, like the time I was playing with my dog, and broke my foot on a chair leg. I had to walk around my low life job at the life insurance company working in the mail room in crutches.

When sad, I didn't eat. I went from one good meal to one tiny meal that I picked around with my fork. I didn't want food anymore. When I was happy, I ate pretty normal. The bulimia and anorexia messed with my neurotransmitters so severely that my mood was either sad, or manic. My weight became controllable; I began logging all my food in the notebook again. The scale started to drop back to 125, then 122. This time, the rising number on the scales set off anorexia.

My regular food log looked like this:

    Breakfast: Water, tea, no cals

Lunch: diet coke, 0 cals, walked around the neighborhood, drank water

Dinner: Fried Rice and chicken with broccoli and tea. 329 cals

When I was having eating disorder issues, it looked like this:

B: Water, Tea, 0 cals,

L: Diet coke, walked around the neighborhood, drank tons of water

D: rice. ½ cup–Cals: 120

The difference was only 200 calories. And I thrived on that amount of food daily.

I made notes in my notebook, like, "Don't eat so damn much, fatty." I scrawled in hard pencil lead,

"Don't fuck up today stupid." I filled my food diary with quotes and notes from the computer message boards that were really beginning to become popular on the early bulletin boards, leading to the internet.

My favorite was: "Do not eat anything unless you know the exact calories in it." And: "Always think in terms what if I were 15 to 20 pounds lighter?"

I read a lot. From the bulletin boards online, to books about bulimia, anorexia, purging, etc…and I read a lot of horror books by my favorite author. I also enjoyed philosophy books and had a copy of *Notes from the Underground* by Nietzsche which kept me occupied. I learned of the philosophers from reading the Kerouac books.

I had books stacked in my bedroom. There wasn't room for shelves.

I began to collect quotes. It started with quotes from Kerouac, then Neal Cassady. Then I gathered lines from song lyrics: Springsteen, Dylan, Grateful Dead, Lennon, and Robert Johnson, Boomtown Rates, Queen, and all the classic songs and performers I valued. Then I began to compile quotes from presidents I admired, then quotes from Rolling Stone interviews, then quotes from artists, quotes from message boards, and quotes from people I heard on TV. I had hundreds of quotes written on 5 x 7-inch paper and placed into a notebook that I categorized. Categorizing wasn't enough, I alphabetized the categories.

I made a cross stitch chart with my favorite Kerouac quote and stitched it on navy blue aida cloth with several variegated DMC colors, meaning each stitch was separate to bring out the color of the thread. Never mind it was a harsh statement and the dark blue aida cloth was a difficult fabric color to even see the dark stitches. I hung it on my wall, and still have it near my bed where I can read it daily.

In the end, I had a notebook full of hundreds of quotes, categorized in alphabetical order. I collected and categorized like a mad man with a goal in mind.

The internet began to change around 1988/89. I noticed more color to the screen, and my mom's house had AOL. I looked on AOL for skinny girl quotes, and pictures, every time I went to her house. I kept collecting and compiling quotes. At the bookstore, I bought books on quotes. I even found quote books of rock musicians, which I bought. For months, I did this activity, as if the quotes were going to die and I was saving them. I read my quote book for years and still have it in my bookcase.

While franticly collecting quotes there was other manic behavior. Manic behavior, anxiety and panic attacks, it's all related to the serotonin depletion. Impulse control is another problem.

In 1988, when my eating disorder was active for example, I'd have a credit card for Macy's, and in one day max it out. When shopping, I visited every department that interested me, and bought whatever it was I wanted, without thought. I had bags and bags from Macy's. When the bill came the next month, I either put it aside, or pay the minimum. The bill came the next month, and I'd do the same.

I received collection calls and screwed up my credit big time. It took me years to rebuild my credit and it's only to the point now where I have a small amount of credit on a card to use on Amazon. If I had had Amazon during my most active phase of the eating disorder, the UPS man could have been busy at my house. I hated collection calls; they drove me insane. The job of a bill collector has got to be the most depressing job that exists.

I had to control my shopping. I started controlling my shopping by either not going, or leaving the card at home, only taking cash.

This was after I spent months making a book of quotes. I began to kind of calm my mania down, either with breath work or beer. But beer had calories so that didn't work well for me.

A treatment (not a cure) for mania phases is a selective serotonin reuptake inhibitor such as Prozac or Zoloft that works by increasing the serotonin levels in the brain, but they are also used to help with eating disorders. Everyone I knew seemed to be on Prozac. At my job the people who worked in the employee claims department were nosey, and no privacy existed. I had to write a claim every time I saw a doctor. It was embarrassing. I preferred being manic and didn't seek treatment for a while.

When I wasn't manic, I was slow and lethargic. I felt like I was wound down from a string that was left twirling. The manic phase I didn't mind as long as I didn't shop, so I cross stitched. I made a large eagle for my dad, a house sampler for my mom, several cross stitches for other people. I cut material for wall hangings and was careful to not go into stores.

My one goal was to learn to knit. I kept trying and didn't succeed until the '90's. I couldn't bring myself to try any more. But when my manic phase was off, I felt like sleeping all day. I had no motivation and ate enough to get by.

During my manic phase I felt happy, content. I read. I walked, though I was starting to get tired of exercise. I think over-exercising day after day for hours can burn someone off of working out for the rest of their lives. I tried joining a gym, and quickly grew tired of it. I had to quit the gym, but they wouldn't stop my monthly membership. My credit was ruined again, and I didn't feel that was my fault.

  I found motivation in my ballet class, again. I could forget how shitty I was feeling. My weight started to go up to 127, almost 130. 130 is a BMI of 24.0, and right at the point of being overweight. It was horrifying, but I wasn't able to control what I ate. On the computer, one could easily find BMI charts, I knew where my numbers stood. When I was manic, I ate anorexic, if I was down, I had to have 3 meals a day.

Chapter 44

APATHY

I got tired of feeling shitty and dragged myself to the doctor. I didn't say a word about the eating disorder, only about depressive symptoms. I won't tell any doctor about my ED. I don't want to turn loose of it even now. I figured the doc would put me on Prozac.

    I was halfway between manic and a downward slide. It was like a tunnel. Doc was awesome, gave me Prozac. Prozac made me tired for weeks, like I had slowed to a stop. I felt robotic. I noticed I ate 3 times a day without thinking about it. Even if I tried to think about food, I ate. On Prozac, I ate a standard American diet without even being aware of eating. At times, I enjoyed what I ate. I kept looking for the response of guilt from eating, which seemed blatantly abnormal and an extreme large amount of food. I lost awareness of my thoughts which were a repeat about food and calories. But I didn't think about calories.

At my job, they ordered pizza. Robotically, I got a paper plate, walked to the pizza boxes, read the type of pizza without thinking and put 2 large pieces on my plate. Then I ate both of them without considering what they would do to my body afterwards. Funny thing, I didn't overeat, I ate what the normal person ate and had no realization that I ate a complete meal. Prozac did something to me where I stopped caring.

My weight went up to 132. 132 is overweight, but when I visited the doctor, he was pleased with my weight. I was fucked up and apathetic. My BMI was an *overweight* BMI, but the doctor was pleased with the number. I told the doctor, "My weight is overweight on the BMI scale." And showed him the scale I had written down in my notebook. I felt my butt and face become round as a large grapefruit. My face puffed out around my eyes. I wanted the thin me back. The thigh gap I loved was gone. My thighs began to heave, and my jean size increased to a 10. And I began to notice. I was about two months into Prozac. I was starting to become slightly aware again.

Granted, the manic phase was gone. In truth, I was balancing, but I hated it. I started to eat energy bars which tasted like grass with honey, organic food, protein shakes which tasted like rocks.

The organic food was taking my entire paycheck and wasn't worth the risk of not paying my bills which piled up but not as bad as when off the Prozac. I took care of bills while on Prozac. Organic food is okay, but it's too expensive to get hung up on. Prozac almost took away my eating disorder, that I connected to and was such a part of me.

On Prozac for about three months, I found I had to make eating decisions. Eating decisions were difficult and time deficient. I would think for hours, 'What am I going to eat tonight?" For lunch, I made it easy, peanut butter sandwiches. For breakfast it was so onerous to wake up, and think, "I'll eat a waffle for breakfast." If I didn't eat three meals, I got so sick, I almost threw up.

My decision making was slow and methodic. Even to the point of when do I go to the grocery store? Grocery stores were easy when the eating disorder was active. When I became manic, life was out of control. On Prozac, nothing motivated me. I had to think while on Prozac, do I need dish soap? Do I need aspirin? Do I need bread?

I lost interest in reading, writing and even stitching for a while. I didn't want to look at quilts. So I sat and watched TV, and ate. My weight went up to 138. I visited the doctor who was pleased, again, with my weight gain, which was the overweight classification on the BMI scale. I was up to size 12 in jeans.

A few times on Prozac I had panic attacks. The first occurred when I had to drive in rain so hard it flooded the roads. I froze and couldn't get in my car but had to go to work. When I got to work, I didn't feel like I accomplished anything great, and dreaded getting into my car after work to drive back to my apartment.

All of my panic attacks had to do with driving. When I was off the Prozac, on the eating disorder, or manic, I never had panic attacks. Granted, I was taking Prozac practically on an empty stomach, which would metabolize the medication in a different manner.

I mentioned the panic attacks to my doctor. He prescribed me Xanax. Xanax is an anti-anxiety medication. When used properly, it is very effective for anxiety and panic attacks.

Between the 2 medications, I was dreadfully numb. Xanax made me sleepy, so I only took it at night.

I started to become irritated, but Prozac was supposed to keep you happy. Fighting the side effects of Prozac, a biggie was weight gain and by now I knew why, I started to count all my food, and go back to one meal a day, and eventually succeeded. I fought the aftereffects of Prozac (nausea, dizziness) and won. No way was I going to fuck up again. My weight began to go down to a more controllable number.

The side effects of Prozac were too much for me, and I stopped taking it, flushing the rest down the toilet. To see me in public, I probably looked normal to anyone. But I when I looked in the mirror, I thought I was puffy, waterlogged, tired looking, pale, and unkempt.

Coming down from Prozac by just stopping isn't a grand idea. Immediately stopping SSRI's, one can experience nausea, headaches, stomach distress, light headedness, and weird vision changes. This is called serotonin syndrome and is a serious condition.

I stopped Prozac on a Friday and took the weekend easy. I didn't trust myself to go anywhere or drive anywhere. The day after stopping it, I sat for hours watching nothing in particular on TV. My inactivity bothered me. On Sunday I tried to go out and walked a little but there was little motivation. Eating decisions were difficult so I kind of gave up on it and ate one meal a day. I was lucky I didn't have any bad symptoms. I had been on Prozac for 5 months.

Chapter 45

DISRUPTING

It became apparent that my job, which was still filing in the basement of a dishonest life insurance company wasn't going anywhere. I began to think about an actual career, when I met Matt. Matt worked in the maintenance department at a large distribution company. He visited the insurance company and made fiddly conversation with me.

I blew it off, "why would he be interested in me? I'm the one they spit out for more serious relationships. Once they are tired of me, that's it." The conversations between Matt and I deepened, and it scared me. I was pretty sure he'd take away my food obsession if I allowed for any sort of relationship.

Occasionally Matt stopped by my apartment. We shared conversations (mostly about concerts we've seen or where we wanted to travel.) I was afraid to invite him for dinner, so we would meet at coffee shops for lunch.

One night he bought pizza after work, when he stopped by my apartment. I was slightly mortified but hid my feelings. The huge pizza in the box, the smell, and even thinking about it brought feelings of dread. He offered me to have a piece "Or two or three, haha."

I timidly selected one small piece.

He said, "Are you hungry?"

I couldn't lie and say I just ate. I had worked all day and had only been home a half an hour. So, I got one piece and started to pick around at it. It had been a few months since I ate in front of anyone. I was eating a very small lunch, and often an apple for dinner. This was my pattern. I knew if I ate any more it would cause problems both with the eating disorder and on the scale. Anything that caused a variation of the pattern could disrupt my whole being, which at this point in my life had to do with controlling Ed with Ana.

So, I chose to eat one piece. And I slowly ate each bite, I noticed I was counting them. Bite counting is going to be discussed later on in this book. Bite counting in 1986 controlled Ed and became my sanity.

"Man, you eat slow. There's plenty, have some more." Matt kept offering. I helped myself to two more slices which surprised me, but it was delicious.

Matt had to work the next day and left the pizza in my refrigerator. "Haha, I'm going to teach you to eat." We hugged and he left.

I closed the door. I had gone against my rules. I looked in my cabinet for Ipecac, because it was my first thought. Why I would think "Ipecac" I'll never know. Karen Carpenter died of using the stuff, and I thought of her. Then I decided to purge the old way.

I hadn't purged since 1984, of course my eating had steadily been controlled so there was no need. I discovered how comforting it was to face my toilet. I knew the tricks to purging. I had plenty of experience. Wet your fingers with warm water. Tickle the top of your esophagus to create a gag reflux. If nothing starts happening, push in your stomach. But whatever happens, don't let food digest.

Then it happened. Out came the chewed up, undigested pizza. It took 5 good purges for success. *Good* meaning, I jammed my fingers (index and middle) down my throat to create a gag reflux so I could expel the chunks of pizza. I did this 5 times. It didn't take care of all the pizza in my stomach, but most. When I was finished, I flushed the toilet, washed my sweaty face and sat down on the bathroom floor. The neurotransmitters bouncing around felt familiar and even refreshing. I smiled with success because I knew tomorrow, I'd not gain any weight. Pizza weight is often from salt and gluten. Pizza is terrifying for someone with an eating disorder.

I rested well that night. The purge provided relaxation. My anxiety was gone. The next morning, I got up, weighed myself and lost 2 pounds. Fuck yeah! 130. I can get down to 125 now. I knew exactly why and knew I could come back to this space at any time. I was glad I dug bulimia out of my head from where it hid. But the disruption to my diet brought on another round of bulimia, like a cruel circle.

I only purged once a week, when I allowed myself to eat more than one meal a day. I did this on purpose so I could keep my neurotransmitters active. My friends noticed I was in control (no manic activity). I dusted! I cleaned. I was happy. Now, when I wasn't bulimic, I was manic after a few days.

Matt and I were getting closer. I knew sex was next. I didn't want to show him my body. What if I had flab, or worse, I'm sure my ribs protruded, I did rib checks in the mirror once a week. My stomach, is it flat? If you think pizza is terrifying to a bulimic girl, having to show your body to a man, is much worse. (This thought would haunt me to the present, when I finally realized men didn't care at a stomach pudge. THAT'S not what they are looking at.)

Granted, I spent hours staring at *thinspo* pictures on the internet. Those girls, perfect. How did they get that way? I felt they were almost sexy, I was not. I was always 10 pounds too heavy. I hadn't any clue they might have been Photoshopped.

Matt kept attempting to persuade me to eat more. It may have been what drove us apart. My mind was constantly obsessing about calories. I couldn't throw myself into a full relationship. We split a few months later. It wasn't exciting or dramatic, we just lost interest.

When Matt and I split, I felt something dark around me. An imaginary wall started to build shading me from people. I started to avoid social interactions. Eye contact always freaked me out, but this was total avoidance. I noticed this right away and visited my physician who gave me a script for Prozac. I'll give it a try, a real sincere attempt this time. I limited my social interactions and gave Prozac another chance. I started to feel in order. (This is the moment that I'm glad my doctor didn't prescribe my favorite of anti-depressants, Wellbutrin. It is an appetite suppressant to some people.)

I visited my mom who ordered pizza. I watched as I ate three pieces without even worrying about the consequences. By the end of the week, I started getting hungry without thoughts of food. This would be a normal person's hunger, but I didn't realize it at the time.

    I went to the grocery store and bought raspberries, oatmeal, chicken. I took them home and cooked chicken.

    I weighed myself and gained seven pounds and blew it off. My size nine jeans were getting tight. I bought a size 11. I bought the size 13 jeans without criticizing myself on the size. I liked to walk everywhere, drive if I had to. As I exercised, I was gaining weight that didn't bother me. I visited the doctor again, and he wrote a prescription for five months of Prozac.

As I lived each day, I didn't contemplate food. I started to enjoy painting and quilting. It was little minor thoughts I had controlled. Eating wasn't one of them. I started eating normal, without breakfast. I never was a fan and still am not. I lived normally for years on Prozac, not aware of how much I gained.

Chapter 46

NORMALCY

I became normal and lived normal. But in 1993, I got tired of being what I called myself a "fat zombie". I took myself off Prozac but still got the prescriptions. Off Prozac I listened to Nirvana. I read ancient Buddhist manuscripts and continued reading Kerouac. I completely identified with Kurt Cobain. I worked and maintained a job, hated social interaction and eye contact and exhibited other behaviors. When I got back to my apartment, I popped a CD into the player. The CD played Nirvana's album *"Nevermind."*

On April 5th, 1994, Cobain's death was on every radio station. I felt crushed and had a meltdown. I went to McDonalds, came home ate and immediately purged until it hurt, and I purged some more. Nirvana was my background music to the darkest part of my brain. Then, shit, what did I do? I brought bulimia back from where it hid. It felt comforting and almost began a habit, but it didn't last. I also used 3-5 laxatives nightly during this time. I lost ten pounds in one month, not a record of course.

A few months later, Fen-Phen was released. I found a doctor who prescribed Fen-Phen. I weighed around 148. My goal weight was…119. No, I think it was lower, 95. Me, off Prozac.

Fen-phen was the true answer. I could go all day, hardly without any food. And I did. And I laughed at my past anorexia which used to be so hard to keep my weight down. The Phen-fen doctor drew my labs. My potassium was dangerously low. I started eating one banana a day and one protein. I also water loaded before my doctor's appointment, so he thought I gained more than I did. Weight was stable, potassium better.

Fen-Phen got my weight down to 135. After 135 the scales wouldn't budge. 135 twice at the weight doctor's office and he refused to prescribe it.

Fen-Phen was pulled from the market. I began to do 700 crunches a day. My stomach was flat. Weight went up to about 142, but I got it down by bite counting.

When my weight went up, I would drop to a dangerously low food consumption. And this was in 1995. I went to my doctor who warned me about gaining any more weight. I complained about feeling dark and unmotivated, and my doctor prescribed Zoloft.

Zoloft made me a zombie, but I ate normal. I went to Wendy's and got a combo meal without thinking and ate the entire thing. I stayed on Zoloft long enough to nix the eating disorder to the point of not fixating on food thoughts. I got tired of being like a zombie and complained to my doctor who didn't prescribe any more Zoloft and shrugged his shoulders.

Except for fragments of discouraging thoughts on food, Zoloft helped tremendously. But my weight increased above 150.

Chapter 47

INTERLUDE NUMBER 150

Around 1997, my weight went up to 150. Becoming concerned, I spent two months bite counting each meal, struggling, and my weight went down to 142.

Year after year I gained ten pounds. I was occasionally able to get the scales down to 145. In 2,000, I was up to 157. Before blaming metabolism which I question, it was food choices and neurotransmitters.

At 160 in 2002, I started bite counting as this was my pattern. It worked as long I kept bite counting. I lost interest and got depressed, again. I went to the doctor and complained, and he gave me Zoloft. He should've given me Wellbutrin as I felt like a lazy slug. I was unhappy with myself when one night I cooked a frozen pizza and ate the entire thing. The reason why people gain weight with Zoloft is the serotonin floating around in the brain. People feel good and forget about how much they eat. This is normal eating?

I stayed on Zoloft and kept my weight where it was. I fought the anti-depressant, starved, bite counted and got accused of "eating like a bird." I maintained no relationship with people and isolated myself.

Chapter 48

THIS IS THE END

In 2004 I took myself off of Zoloft and weighed one morning. On Zoloft I didn't care what I weighed. Filled with apathy, walking around, and not giving a shit. I gained 10 pounds. I checked myself in the mirror, and my gut hung out over my jeans. I began to do 200 crunches because 700 crunches were too difficult. I began to bite count. 15 bites for lunch. 15 bites for dinner. I lost quite a bit of weight. This worked for a while, until I got obsessive about bites. Then I got bored with bite counting.

After Zoloft, Prozac and starving by bite counting, I walked away from anorexia, bulimia and all of the eating disorders. I couldn't do it anymore. I lost my drive. I started eating normally and gained ten pounds.

One last chance, I found a bite counting diet online, started on it, and lost twenty pounds quick. I was doing home workouts, which became popular and hurt my shoulder. Doctor put me on a high dose of Mobic, and I had to eat. There wasn't a choice. I gained 15 pounds, and I was mad. I felt like a weight loss commercial. Except for the metabolism idea of dieting all your life and the weight doesn't come off. I would look at the TV and think, "weight will come off if you force it." I was done forcing it off.

I lost motivation and got depressed. My whole body felt like it was dragging. I stopped running and did nothing but watch TV. I went to my doctor, who put me on Wellbutrin, per my suggestion. In three weeks', time, I lost 10 pounds. I got tasks completed. I started liking people and using eye contact. My friends noticed I was more open and receptive.

On Welbutrin, I was wearing a size twelve jeans. I worked out at a gym not compulsively, and I walked or ran a mile a day unless it rained. I was a continuous battery that stayed motivated. I made quilts. I attended social events and tried not to isolate myself. My doctor was glad I lost ten pounds.

Chapter 49

I'M ALIVE, AND SO AND SO

Five years later, I was alive. Fuck those diet commercials, the skinny lingerie models and striving for a size 6. I found my size 7 hellacious, imagine a size 6?

I was on Welbutrin and I loved it. It helped me through a major job lay-off that I could've handled much worse. I occasionally went to a Buddhist center and had a few friends. I ran as many 5k's as I could (correction, walked them). I didn't care if I wasn't number one or perfect.

When I accidently forgot to refill my Wellbutrin after three weeks, I become a slug. I complained about this to my doctor who said, "Then remember to renew it, and continue to run. Oh, and loose a few pounds."

Lose a few pounds. The words make my bones chill. Anyone else would say, "Oh can you help me with that too?" I couldn't say those words and didn't care to start another diet. It made me ill to think of trying to start another diet.

I looked back on my failed eating disorder. It wasn't difficult to lose weight the way I chose; it wasn't a form of dieting or weight loss at all. Anorexia isn't the easy way out. It's a mental illness. It made me mad that no health professional recognized I was sick in college and diagnosed it. I could've been treated by a therapist who helped me with actual treatment than the crap I had to endure. Granted, I manipulated a therapist. I just wanted to be thin enough to be diagnosed with anorexia. Then it escalated into bulimia which I hid. And I was sick.

I'm sure if I had the behavior in 2022 and was twenty years old, it would immediately be a concern. I don't believe I'd be able to keep anorexia or bulimia concealed. It's common and people are educated. I do think that there should be more education about adults with eating disorders, or even those over 150 pounds, or with a BMI 28.9-39.

Every day of my life I thought about anorexia, and even the worst, bulimia. I weighed myself and got mad if I gain, happy if I lost. Wellbutrin helped not focusing on the scales. I tried on my size ten jeans and got irritated when they fit too tight. (I own them for *thinspiration*.) I'll kept trying to know I will succeed. Maybe I'll get down to 119. In an ap on my iPhone, that's my "accomplished weight." 119!! No, I really want to be skinnier, 95 pounds. That's my mindset. I put aside the disorder somewhere in the brain but dig out the thought, not the action. The action is eating a little less than I should because I want to get my weight down and the numbers on the scales to drop.

    Eventually I had to stop the Wellbutrin, it made me irritated. I never returned to it.

Chapter 50

A LOOK BACK

As I sit here thinking of the little girl who looked 12, the young woman, myself, at 18 or 20 years old, it feels like I wrote a fictional story. Was that really me? How could I had been so tiny and endured what I withstood for years? I can't understand the anguish I put myself through, and how it developed into years of dangerous ideas and scary health risks.

    I described everything with as much detail as I could, grotesque to the point of the smell. I can still feel the grease on my fingers from purging cake with chocolate icing thirty-five years ago. It's gross, but I can't simply wipe the memory away.

I know I messed up my neurotransmitters, from feeling like crap to feeling okay and always with a little apathy. I don't get excited about things. I stare and scowl but continue to be motivated. When I'm happy, though, it shows. I've not felt manic for a few years, and that's a blessing. I'm unorganized, sometimes complacent but controlled.

I say I failed an eating disorder because I never got to ninety-five pounds. That's the eating disorder whispering in my ear from my past. In fact, when I describe this book to people, I'm forthcoming, "It's about my failed eating disorder." People raise an eyebrow; make a weird expression, then say, "Hmm. To fail an eating disorder means you die." Not to me. It's a feeling of unsuccessful abandon. It failed me when I walked away from it.

At first it seems funny to people when they hear about a failed eating disorder. It's not funny at all. I read about girls all the time that do the same thing I did and are skinnier than ninety-five pounds. Some get dangerously low, below eighty pounds. The BMI charts say ninety-five is almost perfect. What I'd give now to experience the weight of ninety-five pounds.

Why not try a diet? Eating disorders are not a diet. Why not try the Ana rules to keep the weight off? I know the rules well. Just that mindset is sickening but raw with honesty and never vanishes. It's too easy to return to cheese and peanut butter crackers, that are now 200 calories, and a calorie free drink. There are several drinks available with vitamins. Some bottled drinks have a little caffeine, and five calories.

Protein bars are premade perfection for calorie counting. The words, "Meal Replacement" on a box of protein bars cause me to cringe. We already know what bars are used for. Bars work great, exactly like cheese and peanut butter crackers and Tab. It worked for me many years ago, kept me skinny. Counting calories is easy with protein bars. Read the labels, there's tons of vitamins, supplements, "super food", fruits, and claims they contain a day's serving of food. It's easy to go back to old tricks of calorie counting, one meal a day, and equivalent to what I consumed.

Fasting diets, intermittent fasting, juice fasts, water fasts which encompasses less food than someone *with* anorexia consumes; these types of diets are pushed into popularity by the internet, books and articles. People with anorexia are smart enough to know to eat just enough food to not be weak or pass out. Once anorexia victims reach that phase, they are truly sick. Fasting is temporary and will make someone sick if it's done for longer than a week or two. The danger with some of these diets is if one tries juice fasting or worse, water fasting, and are not experienced, it can make them ill. If a person has no idea to eat enough so they don't pass out, the results can be chaos. A severe calorie deficit is dangerous.

  I've had Ana nudge me recently. But calorie counting, restricting, bite counting, fasting, liquid fasting, one meal a day, cheese and peanut butter crackers, nutrition bars, meal replacement bars, the smoothie diet, then purging (it's on the end of the list.

It's the other part of the story.) Where's the end? I failed my eating disorder which I still own. What I didn't fail was life. I have a great son, my mom and friends and friends at work. I'm a nurse. My pregnancy was never a part of this story. It was the opposite of this. It is a different path. My painting sometimes is weird. I think walking or running is meditative.

For activities, I run. Every workout has to do with improving running. None of my exercises are compulsive. My body isn't perfect. I drool when the tummy tuck commercial comes on TV because I want one. I want the gastric balloon. I want a lap band. I still want to be skinny. I want to be ninety-five pounds! It's success. I can't bring myself to stick my finger down my throat, but if overindulging in a yummy meal, feeling uncomfortable and full, the thought enters my brain and I wasn't beyond the act. I admit here that I have purged, especially during a relapse. I talk openly about it, and my friends know. It needs to be talked about, and not just about me.

I have about 45 more years to live. Eating disorders can strike anyone, at any time in their lives if they are predisposed. It's not worth my time to go too far trying to stay skinny.

I spent years eating 500 calories a day and I'm tired of thinking about calories, but I still track my food. Tracking food for me is dangerous. I just want to enjoy food for once. I know the exact amount of most of the calories I eat. It's a grey area. If yogurt is around 100 calories, cheese and peanut butter crackers are 200. There are no calories in La Croix, but a banana has 105. Apples contain 95 calories. The obsession starts, and it doesn't stop without stopping my thoughts. Skittles have 4 calories a piece. If there's 4 calories a piece in one Skittle, 10 is a whopping 40 calories. Calories are great for the mind to catalogue.

I think about the food I consume on a daily basis. But I get hungry and try to eat it anyway. I try to go without food, but I can't think clearly. And so many years ago, I was like a battery, constantly denying my needs for food and nutrients. What did anorexia and bulimia do for me? What did it provide me? What gifts did they bring?

My eating disorder put me in a private hell. That little voice of Ana still exists. She's in my brain and I wonder if she'll be there the rest of my life.

I don't *need* Ana. Yet I created her and own her.

Afterword Gateway from Hell

I run numerous 5Ks', but sometimes running doesn't help the feelings of inadequacy. Ana (or worse) is there but I'm not sure anyone understands. I have a few close friends: Ambre, Luke, Becca. Celeste and Miles. Ambre, Becca, Luke and Miles are running friends but became my best friends. Ambre is an amazing friend, who runs faster than I do. She's stunning. Literally my spirit animal. She's everything I'd want to be, beautiful, caring and fun. Her hair flows in long brown curly waves, much like mine but longer. Ambre and I do a lot of non-running activities and occasionally go out and listen to a

Grateful Dead tribute band. Ambre runs half and full marathons and wins her age group every time.

My friend Luke and I talk a lot at running events and on social media. He's an incredible person and gives so much of himself.

Becca and I share deep dark secrets. She runs my pace but has done a few marathons. I have not done half or full marathons, my turn is coming. Becca is almost like a coach to me during the race, but she's also a very good friend off the race. I've confided in Becca on several occasions, often the bad before the good.

Celeste runs ultras. She is my hair goal. Her hair curls like mine but is much longer. She is highly prized and known in the metaphysical world. I've been friends with her for years. She helped me with Lady Ana when I first had the brilliant idea to write my own anorexia story out of desperation for the crap I kept seeing on TV. "I'll just write my own, this is how it really is." She understands that this is how it is. I wrote the book to maintain the grotesque visuals that bulimia and anorexia brings. I took the magic out of it. She accepted that it was honest, down to the smell which is putrid. She's behind me every step of this book.

  I'm closest to Miles without allowing myself to become clingy. I like observing boundaries and appreciate the slight distance. Boundaries allow me to control what I still have. Miles also runs half marathons and marathons. He lives a few blocks from my home, and I tend to load my crap on him. I'm protective of what I used to be, and I'm always vigilant. I've always been spit out by men, so I'm used to whatever comes around. I question if humans love each other, or do they like each other and if love is fake. I'm very protective of this, and it's probably from past experiences with anorexia when my head wasn't screwed on tight. I don't know where this feeling comes from. I'm glad Miles gets it and knows how I feel. I'm glad he doesn't take me too seriously. That would be atrocious. I've chose to confide in him on a few things, without being attached. Miles will never spit me out. He's present. He lives in the present and never looks in the past. I've shared with him parts of my life, all except for the worse of this book. Nobody knows the worse except for Celeste.

    At races, I look for Miles first. He's easy to spot, dark brown soft hair, deep brown eyes, green shorts and a grey hydration vest that he hates. Then I find Ambre, Becca and Luke. Becca is usually talking to her friends. I often see Luke early enough. Ambre sashays into the race before it starts. Besides close friends, they will lift a person up when needed. I never had anyone I could confide in except my piano teacher, Calvin, and I should've taken his lead, and not created this whole mess.

My biggest issue about races is eating. Understandable, but could become a problem. Again, I'm very protective of it, and I'm not getting rid of the defense mechanism. My biggest triumph was stepping on the scales and losing 11 pounds in a month from sweat, but I know in my heart I skipped a few meals. Sssh, no one knows and it's okay. And who is that talking? Ana.

Always on the verge of a relapse, everything is a cautious step. I like to be close to people, but unsure of what to do or how to be a friend. My friends are patient and helpful and I'm grateful. I'm behind my friends 100% and am very lucky to have them. In relapse, I hate being around groups of people.

In 2021, I felt Ana lurking. I could feel her churn in my thought process again. Another fucking relapse. I tried a macro counting diet coach and had to count and log everything I put into my mouth. (fats, carbs, sodium, cholesterol, calories, every little bite that went into my mouth.) I made a goal to beat the macro count. (Sounds like me back in college). I brought my calories down to 900 a day, even though I run or walk 2-3 miles 3 times a week. I felt like shit. I beat my macros daily by eating less than suggested. Everything declined until Ana had me blocked in a corner. I was down to 850 calories a day. I continued running; I was working out at a popular fitness gym and in these activities, I burned 450 calories each time.

I was so proud that I beat my macros. I started to lie on the coach food log, and my macros coach believed me. My friends thought I was doing great! My waist was narrowing. I weighed myself once a day at first, then 2 times a day, in the morning, then after my workout. Tick Tock Tick Tock…. Let's try 800 calories a day, logging double the amount of food for my macros coach, logging single in a little notebook of my own. It worked great! Albeit probably not ideal.

I went to a new doctor. My labs were off. Tick Tock. Ana sat in the corner glaring at me. I was able to correct my labs with diet, then I realized something felt wrong, mentally. My eating disorder always made me feel like I was standing in a warp or sitting in an air tunnel. When I felt the air tunnel, I'd know that Ana was sneaking up behind me with guilt. When I noticed this feeling, I fired my macros coach. I could feel the tunnel!

After firing my coach, I had to pull myself out of the fucking hole again. It wasn't an easy thing to do, and it wasn't pleasant. I avoided people. I tried to avoid meals. I fought urges to eat but little by little, I dragged myself out of the goddamn mess, and thought I was a winner. I had no idea what kind of winner, I didn't defeat anything. Eventually, my new doctor put me on Lexapro because I had a panic attack in a parking lot. Lexapro worked wonders, until it caused anxiety.

About 6 months later beginning of 2022, I went through *another* dark time. While running, I noticed my wrist scar from when I was 16 and wanted to die. My scar began to show. I hadn't noticed it as strong before.

Then I realized I was never treated for the eating disorder, for all of THIS in this book.

    I drove the short drive to Mile's house almost out of my mind blaming other people because no one helped me. At least he didn't turn me away, other people would I'm sure, except my friends. I have no idea why I turned to him. He helped me become grounded, and we talked. It was all about me, but maybe it needed to be. But I felt selfish being all about me. I learned I can't live in that space. Yet I fight it daily. Not treated? I should investigate that. But fighting it, I'm alive. My next tattoo should be a small semicolon, and ----Cut on thin line--- on my ankle. I now have friends who kind of understand, if they knew the whole story.

While going over the words of this book, Ana caused a serious relapse. I'd go out for breakfast, eat one pancake and that is all for the day. I thought 1 pancake for a day's worth of food, after a 5K was okay. I lied to everyone but Miles, about what I ate. If I only ate a pancake, I said I had a huge dinner. It became a dangerous pattern. I didn't realize the pattern, until one night, I thought about my food consumption. Not being someone who cries, I cried for 4 nights. I didn't know what to do. Ana wouldn't stop. I finally admitted it to Miles, with a fuckable "Deer in the headlights" look of depression and shame, and an expression that abolished further morals.

I lost 14 pounds in 3 ½ weeks, 20 pounds in about 2 months. I weighed myself daily, and after races. Weight increases were not allowed, no matter what it took. If I ate "too much" I purged. I bought cake or cupcakes for the purpose of purging. It is easy as an adult, no one is staring at you. If a friend asked how I lost the weight, I turned to them and shook my head, "no." Yet I was complimented for my weight loss and people asked my secrets.

I STILL have a clavicle goal, and I'm starting to notice achievement in that category.

I'm not cured. In fact, sometimes, some days, I feel worthless but I'm okay. EVERYTHING'S FINE!! I often think, what if I was treated, how would I view life; how would I view food and nutrients? I guess I'll never know. Living in the unknown seems to be the jargon of my life and mental wellbeing, and physical wellbeing is questionable. Running hardly helps with mental well-being. Talking about it, if I admit it, helps a lot.

My secret is told. For this part of my life, the book is closed. While I own my failed eating disorder and the pathway of Lady Ana, she doesn't own me.

At least my story's not over. A semi-colon ends a sentence and starts another. I'm waiting for the other sentence to begin.

After Thought

If you have a problem with eating or any of the issues I've described, don't wait to seek help. Do it. Don't let this be an example. Anorexia and bulimia are not worth holding onto. But they are worth letting go.

References

Body Mass Index Table 1. (n.d.). Retrieved from https://www.nhlbi.nih.gov/health/educational/lose_wt/BMI/bmi_tbl.htm

Eating disorders - Eating Disorders - NCBI Bookshelf. (2004). Retrieved from https://www.ncbi.nlm.nih.gov/books/NBK49318/

Eating Disorders Statistics and Information. (2018). Retrieved from https://www.mirror-mirror.org/eating-disorders-statistics.htm

Ekern, J. (2018, February 11). Dental Problems Caused by Bulimia. Retrieved from https://www.eatingdisorderhope.com/information/bulimia/dental-problems-caused-by-bulimia

Glossary. (2017, March 22). Retrieved from https://www.nationaleatingdisorders.org/learn/glossary

Haelle, T. (2013, September 25). Expanded Clinical Definition of Anorexia May Help More Teens. Retrieved from https://www.scientificamerican.com/article/expanded-clinical-definition-of-anorexia-may-help-more-teens/

Lauren Muhlheim, PsyD, CEDS. (2016, October 12). Chew and Spit Is a Lesser-Known Behavior in Eating Disorders. Retrieved from https://www.verywellmind.com/chew-and-spit-eating-disorder-behavior-4100664

Malik M, et al. (n.d.). Rectal prolapse associated with bulimia nervosa: report of seven cases. - PubMed - NCBI. Retrieved from https://www.ncbi.nlm.nih.gov/pubmed/9369117

Music Therapist Employment Outlook | CareersinPsychology.org. (n.d.). Retrieved from https://careersinpsychology.org/employment-outlook-guidance-musical-therapists/

Neurotransmitters. (2016, December 21). Retrieved from https://www.nationaleatingdisorders.org/toolkit/parent-toolkit/neurotransmitters

Steinkellner, K. (2014, July 2). The Scary History Behind 'Thinspiration'. Retrieved from https://hellogiggles.com/beauty/scary-history-behind-thinspiration/

Triggers - Eating Disorders Glossary. (n.d.). Retrieved from http://glossary.feast-ed.org/5-psychology-and-therapies/triggers

https://www.eatingdisorderhope.com/blog/genetic-factors-eating-disorders

South Eastern Centre Against Sexual Assault & Family Violence. (n.d.). Feelings after sexual assault. Retrieved from https://www.secasa.com.au/pages/feelings-after-sexual-assault/

Watson, G. (n.d.). Body Mass Index (BMI) Chart. Retrieved from https://256stuff.com/gray/docs/body_mass_index_bmi.html

Your Body's Response to Chewing and Spitting: The Role of Insulin. (2015, September 7). Retrieved from https://www.scienceofeds.org/2013/03/21/your-bodys-response-to-chewing-and-spitting-the-role-of-insulin/

About the author

Rhonda lives in Independence, MO with her dog and her mom. She has an adult son who is married. His wife and him have a beautiful son. Rhonda is an LPN and works for a great company with the best co-workers. She runs most 5K's, a few 10K' s in Kansas City, and the next step is a few half marathons. Her friends, who names and appearance she changed are supportive. She remains closest to Miles and Ambre. Rhonda makes legacy and journey hand bound journals, reads Kerouac, Edgar Allan Poe and collects oddities. She listens to the Grateful Dead among others. She is thankful for what she has achieved.

Rhonda is looking forward to finishing her second book, "Unharmonious Running." And is creating a 100 night poem project.

www.ingramcontent.com/pod-product-compliance
Lightning Source LLC
Chambersburg PA
CBHW031130160426
43193CB00008B/92